TEACHER'S PET PUBLICATIONS

LITPLAN TEACHER PACK
for
Tears of a Tiger
based on the book by
Sharon M. Draper

Written by
Christina Wulff

© 2009 Teacher's Pet Publications
All Rights Reserved

ISBN 978-1-60249-703-0

Copyright Teacher's Pet Publications 2009

Only the student materials in this unit plan (such as worksheets, study questions, and tests) may be reproduced multiple times for use in the purchaser's classroom.

For any additional copyright questions, contact Teacher's Pet Publications.

www.tpet.com

TABLE OF CONTENTS - *Tears of a Tiger*

About The Author	5
Introduction	7
Unit Objectives	9
Reading Assignment Sheet	10
Unit Outline	11
Study Questions (Short Answer)	15
Quiz/Study Questions (Multiple Choice)	25
Pre-reading Vocabulary Worksheets	47
Lesson One (Introductory Lesson)	63
Raising Awareness Project	65
Non-Fiction Assignment Sheet	69
Oral Reading Evaluation Sheet	76
Writing Assignment 1	79
Writing Assignment 2	88
Extra Writing Assignments/Discussion ?s	91
Writing Assignment 3	104
Vocabulary Review Activities	106
Unit Review Activities	107
Unit Tests	113
Unit Resource Materials	169
Vocabulary Resource Materials	189

ABOUT THE AUTHOR

Sharon M. Draper

Sharon Draper was born in Cleveland, Ohio. Her parents stressed the importance of reading and a strong education, resulting in Draper becoming an excellent student and a self-proclaimed bookworm. Draper was awarded the National Merit Scholarship based on her high SAT scores and headed to Pepperdine University to fulfill her childhood dream of becoming a teacher. She graduated with a degree in English and moved back to Ohio to obtain her master's degree at Miami University of Ohio.

As a teacher in Cincinnati, Ohio, Draper was known for the high expectations she held for all her students. The senior research paper she assigned was so tough, it became legendary. Students who survived the "Draper Paper" were awarded a t-shirt. After years of encouraging her students to submit their stories and poems to writing contests, a student approached Draper and told her she should do the same. Draper followed through with the challenge and was awarded first place for her short story "One Small Torch" in an annual contest held by *Ebony* magazine.

From there, Draper's writing career began. Draper sought to write literature that teens could relate to and enjoy. Since then she has published several young adult novels and children's books, receiving multiple awards for her writing.

Tears of a Tiger is the first book in the Hazelwood High trilogy. The main character in the second title in the series, *Forged by Fire*, is Gerald Nickelby, one of Andy's basketball teammates. *Darkness Before Dawn* follows Andy's girlfriend, Keisha, through her senior year of high school.

Major Works
Tears of a Tiger Forged by Fire Darkness Before Dawn
Romiette and Julio Double Dutch The Battle of Jericho
Copper Sun November Blues
Fire from the Rock We Beat the Street Teaching from the Heart
Not Quite Burned Out But Crispy Around the Edges
Ziggy and the Black Dinosaurs: The Buried Bones Mystery
Ziggy and the Black Dinosaurs: Lost in the Tunnel of Time
Ziggy and the Black Dinosaurs: Shadows of Caesar's Creek
Ziggy and the Black Dinosaurs: The Space Mission Adventure
Ziggy and the Black Dinosaurs: The Backyard Zoo Adventure
Ziggy and the Black Dinosaurs: Stars and Sparks on Stage

Awards
National Teacher of the Year
Five-time winner of the Coretta Scott King Literary Award
New York Times bestselling author
Excellence in Education Award

Milken Family Foundation National Educator Award
YWCA Career Woman of Achievement
Dean's Award from Howard University School of Education
Pepperdine University Distinguished Alumnus Award
Marva Collins Education Excellence Award
Ohio Pioneer in Education by the Ohio State Department of Education
Governor's Educational Leadership Award

INTRODUCTION *Tears of a Tiger*

This LitPlan has been designed to develop students' reading, writing, thinking, and language skills through exercises and activities related to *Tears of a Tiger*. It includes twenty-two lessons, supported by extra resource materials.

The **introductory lesson** prompts students to think about tragic accidents with teens, one of the topics discussed in the novel.

The **reading assignments** are approximately thirty pages each; some are a little shorter while others are a little longer. Students have approximately 15 minutes of pre-reading work to do prior to each reading assignment. This pre-reading work involves reviewing the study questions for the assignment and doing some vocabulary work for selected vocabulary words they will encounter in their reading.

The **study guide questions** are fact-based questions; students can find the answers to these questions right in the text. These questions come in two formats: short answer or multiple choice. The best use of these materials is probably to use the short answer version of the questions as study guides for students (since answers will be more complete), and to use the multiple choice version for occasional quizzes.

The **vocabulary work** is intended to enrich students' vocabularies as well as to aid in the students' understanding of the book. Prior to each reading assignment, students will complete a two-part worksheet for selected vocabulary words in the upcoming reading assignment. Part I focuses on students' use of general knowledge and contextual clues by giving the sentence in which the word appears in the text. Students are then to write down what they think the words mean based on the words' usage. Part II nails down the definitions of the words by giving students dictionary definitions of the words and having students match the words to the correct definitions based on the words' contextual usage. Students should then have an understanding of the words when they meet them in the text.

After each reading assignment, students will go back and formulate answers for the study guide questions. Discussion of these questions serves as a **review** of the most important events and ideas presented in the reading assignments.

After students complete reading of the work, there is a **vocabulary review** lesson which pulls together all of the fragmented vocabulary lists for the reading assignments and gives students a review of all of the words they have studied.

Following the vocabulary review, a lesson is devoted to the **extra discussion questions**. These questions focus on interpretation, critical analysis and personal response, employing a variety of thinking skills and adding to the students' understanding of the novel.

There is a **Raising Awareness Project** in this unit. This project requires students to conduct research on a topic discussed in the novel and create a way to help increase awareness throughout the school community on the chosen subject.

There are three **writing assignments** in this unit, each with the purpose of informing, persuading, or expressing personal opinions. The first writing assignment asks students to mimic the style of writing found in the novel by conveying information through various perspectives and mediums. The second writing assignment asks students to explain the importance of good communication between parents and teens. In the third assignment students must persuade a fellow teen to get help with a problem he or she is facing.

There is a non-fiction **reading assignment**. Students must read non-fiction articles, books, etc. to gather information about their themes discussed in the novel.

The **review lesson** pulls together all of the aspects of the unit. The teacher is given four or five choices of activities or games to use which all serve the same basic function of reviewing all of the information presented in the unit.

The **unit test** comes in two formats: multiple choice or short answer. As a convenience, two different tests for each format have been included. There is also an advanced short answer unit test for advanced students.

There are additional **support materials** included with this unit. The **Unit Resource Materials** section includes suggestions for an in-class library, crossword and word search puzzles related to the novel, and extra worksheets. There is a list of **bulletin board ideas** which gives the teacher suggestions for bulletin boards to go along with this unit. In addition, there is a list of **extra class activities** the teacher could choose from to enhance the unit or as a substitution for an exercise the teacher might feel is inappropriate for his/her class. **Answer keys** are located directly after the **reproducible student materials** throughout the unit. The **Vocabulary Resource Materials** section includes similar worksheets and games to reinforce the vocabulary words.

The **level** of this unit can be varied depending upon the criteria on which the individual assignments are graded, the teacher's expectations of his/her students in class discussions, and the formats chosen for the study guides, quizzes and test. If teachers have other ideas/activities they wish to use, they can usually easily be inserted prior to the review lesson.

The student materials may be reproduced for use in the teacher's classroom without infringement of copyrights. No other portion of this unit may be reproduced without the written consent of Teacher's Pet Publications.

UNIT OBJECTIVES *Tears of a Tiger*

1. Through reading the novel *Tears Of A Tiger*, students will learn about the way choices made by teens can impact a community and alter the lives of others.

2. Students will learn about some problems teens face and effective ways to handle difficult situations.

3. Students will demonstrate their understanding of the text on four levels: factual, interpretive, critical, and personal.

4. Students will make connections with the material in the text and apply the lessons learned to their lives.

5. Students will be given the opportunity to practice reading aloud and silently to improve their skills in each area.

6. Students will answer questions to demonstrate their knowledge and understanding of the main events and characters in *Tears of a Tiger* as they relate to the author's theme development.

7. Students will enrich their vocabularies and improve their understanding of the novel through the vocabulary lessons prepared for use in conjunction with the novel.

8. Students will demonstrate the ability to write effectively to inform by developing and organizing facts to convey information. Students will demonstrate the ability to write effectively to persuade by selecting and organizing relevant information, establishing an argumentative purpose, and by designing an appropriate strategy for an identified audience. Students will demonstrate the ability to write effectively to express personal ideas by selecting a form and its appropriate elements.

9. Students will read aloud, report, and participate in large and small group discussions to improve their public speaking and personal interaction skills.

READING ASSIGNMENTS *Tears of a Tiger*

Date Assigned	Assignment	Completion Date
	Assignment 1 Crash, Fire, Pain- "Hey, Coach! Can We Talk?"	
	Assignment 2 Sad Songs, Juicy Gossip-Ferocious Frustration	
	Assignment 3 Female Frustration-Black on White	
	Assignment 4 Accepting Fear-The Importance of Friendship	
	Assignment 5 Concern and Denial-Slipping Away	
	Assignment 6 A Father's Dream-End of Novel	

UNIT OUTLINE *Tears of a Tiger*

1 Introduction Activity Project Assignment PVR1	2 Study Questions 1 Vocabulary 1 Character Cut Outs	3 Non-fiction Assignment PVR2	4 Study Questions 2 Vocabulary 2 Inferences/Venn Diagram	5 Teen Psychology Cause & Effect PVR3
6 Study Questions 3 Vocabulary 3 Oral Reading PVR4	7 Speaker	8 Writing #1	9 Study Questions 4 Vocabulary 4 Discrimination	10 Poetry & Perspectives PVR5
11 Study Questions 5 Vocabulary 5 Andy's Personalities PVR6	12 Study Questions 6 Vocabulary 6 Cause & Effect	13 Timeline	14 Talk Show	15 Writing #2
16 Extra Discussion Questions	17 Extra Discussion Questions Cont. Letter to Author	18 Project Presentations Unit Evaluation	19 Writing #3	20 Vocabulary Review
21 Unit Review	22 Unit Test			

Key: P = Preview Study Questions   V = Vocabulary Work   R = Read

STUDY GUIDE QUESTIONS

STUDY GUIDE QUESTIONS *Tears of a Tiger*

Assignment 1
Crash, Fire, Pain- "Hey, Coach! Can We Talk?"

1. According to the newspaper account, what happened on the evening of November 8th?
2. Describe the relationship between Andy and Rob as shown in their conversation after the basketball game on November 7th.
3. Describe the relationship between Andy and Keisha based on Andy's comments after the game on November 7th.
4. Why doesn't Gerald go riding with his friends after the game?
5. How does Keisha respond to the news about the accident and Rob's death in her phone conversation with Rhonda?
6. Tyrone's statement to the police after the accident included many details about that evening. In five sentences or less, summarize the most important facts Tyrone gives the police.
7. B.J. was the only one not drinking on the night of the accident. Later, he feels guilty and wonders if he should have stopped them from driving or offered to drive. What reason does he give for not speaking up?
8. List the questions B.J. asks in his first prayer following the accident.
9. What is Rhonda's most frightening moment?
10. What articles are in the *Herald*'s special edition? List their titles and write one sentence telling what each was about.
11. What are three points Andy makes when he talks to the coach on his first day back to school after the accident?

Assignment 2
Sad Songs, Juicy Gossip-Ferocious Frustration

1. Rhonda mentions that grief counselors have come to the school to help students deal with the accident. What does she say really helps students the most in dealing with Rob's death?
2. What three things would Gerald get rid of if he could change the world? Tell why he would get rid of each.
3. How does Andy's personality change following the accident? What do his friends begin to notice about him?
4. Who takes Rob's old position on the basketball court as center?
5. Andy is outstanding in the first basketball game after the accident. After the game, Coach tells Andy, "Without you, we'd fall apart." What is Andy's response?
6. Rob's parents attend the first game after the accident. What effect does this have on the team and on Andy?
7. How does Andy describe his relationship with his family to his psychologist?
8. What is Keisha's response when Andy invites her to ride on the bus with him out to the mall to see a movie? Why is this response significant?
9. Why does Andy choose to let his grades slide?

Assignment 3
Female Frustration-Black on White

1. Why does Keisha call her mother to come pick her and Andy up at the mall?
2. The December 20th assignments give us important information about each character and touch on many themes in the novel. What are the last two lines of each person's poem?
3. Andy tells his psychologist about being the victim of black stereotyping while shopping at the mall. What does he say used to happen when he and Rob would go shopping?
4. When Dr. Carrothers asks Andy how his trip to the mall with Keisha went, what is Andy's response?
5. Andy tells Dr. Carrothers that Keisha is there for him when no one else is. What examples does he give to show that she is "there for him"?
6. Why doesn't Rob's mother mention "the rock" when she calls Andy on Christmas day?
7. Ms. Blackwell reads the poem "One Thousand Nine Hundred Sixty-Eight Winters" to the class. What is each student's response to the poem? Include responses by Andy, Gerald, Mary Alice, and Keisha.
8. When Andy tells Keisha he is being driven crazy by the thought of Robbie being cold out in the cemetery, what is Keisha's response?

Assignment 4
Accepting Fear-The Importance of Friendship

1. What did Andy do when he and Keisha took a walk out to the freeway, and what was Keisha's response?
2. What promise does Dr. Carrothers make Andy agree to during their therapy session?
3. What does Andy tell Keisha he sees in his future?
4. What does Rob tell Andy in the dream Andy has?
5. What does Andy say in his letter to Rob's parents?
6. When B.J. and Tyrone are concerned about Andy and go to talk to the school counselor about him, what is her response to their concerns?
7. What does Andy tell Dr. Carrothers about Rob's dad's response to the letter?
8. What does Andy say to Dr. Carrothers to convince the doctor that he has improved enough to have appointments on an as-needed basis?
9. What main points does Keisha make in her homework essay about the importance of friendship?
10. What is B.J.'s summary of *Macbeth*, and what is Andy's reaction to it?

Assignment 5
Concern and Denial-Slipping Away
1. When Andy's teacher calls home to alert his parents that Andy could be in real trouble, what is Andy's father's response?
2. Why does Monty put tears on his tiger?
3. In the conversation between two teachers on February 25th, one teacher raises concerns about Andy and asks, "How could he be stable after only three months?" What is the second teacher's response?
4. In her diary entry on March 9th, Keisha says Andy has his parents, teachers, and counselor all fooled into thinking he is adjusting well. According to Keisha, who is the only person who knows how troubled Andy really is? 5. What happens during the talent show when Andy tells Keisha that she sometimes gets on his nerves?
5. What happens during the talent show when Andy tells Keisha that she sometimes gets on his nerves?
6. Andy talks to his mother after the talent show, to try to explain to her how he feels. To what does he compare his feelings?
7. How does Andy's mother respond when Andy asks for help handling the accident?
8. After finding out he missed his opportunity with the basketball scouts, to what conclusion does Andy come?
9. Describe Rhonda and Tyrone's relationship.
10. Rhonda tells Saundra all about Keisha and Andy's breaking up. What is Rhonda's final comment before going on to talk about her prom dress?

Assignment 6
A Father's Dream-End of Novel
1. When Andy's father threatens to punish his son if he doesn't get his grades up, how does Andy respond?
2. Why does Andy's father always call him "Andrew"?
3. Which three people does Andy try to call before he kills himself, and what response does he get from each?
4. Why does Andy think tigers have it rough?
5. How does Andy kill himself?
6. What does Monty see on the ceiling?
7. Why is Tyrone mad at the suicide prevention/grief counseling woman at their school?
8. What does the grief counselor suggest Andy's friends should do to try to work through their pain and frustration over Andy's death?
9. How do each of Andy's friends react to his suicide?
10. What does Monty say he will never forget?
11. When Monty goes to visit Andy's grave, he tells Andy how things have changed since he went away. How has the family changed?

STUDY GUIDE QUESTIONS ANSWER KEY *Tears of a Tiger*

Assignment 1
Crash, Fire, Pain- "Hey, Coach! Can We Talk?"

1. According to the newspaper account, what happened on the evening of November 8th? *Andy Jackson was driving drunk while three friends rode with him in the car. Two of the friends, B.J. and Tyrone, were not injured; however, Robbie was trapped in the car as the engine caught fire.*

2. Describe the relationship between Andy and Rob as shown in their conversation after the basketball game on November 7th.
   It is clear that Rob and Andy are close friends through their friendly teasing back and forth. The two play off of each other well in boasting about the game, and they discuss a variety of issues, such as grades, parents, and girls in their short conversation.

3. Describe the relationship between Andy and Keisha based on Andy's comments after the game on November 7th.
   Though Andy is bragging about his relationship with Keisha, it is obvious from the teasing of the other boys that Keisha has the upper hand in the relationship. It is also made known that Keisha is very important to Andy since he is easily distracted by her throughout the game.

4. Why doesn't Gerald go riding with his friends after the game?
   Gerald hints that his father is strict and says he must hurry home after the game to avoid a more serious situation.

5. How does Keisha respond to the news about the accident and Rob's death in her phone conversation with Rhonda?
   Keisha is worried about all four of the boys and hopes they are all okay. When she discovers Rob died in the accident, she has a hard time dealing with the news and tells Rhonda she's never known anyone who has died before, except her grandmother who was old. Keisha seems to be more concerned with how she and Rhonda will handle the death of a friend rather than being worried about how this will affect Andy after having just watched his friend die in an accident that could have been avoided. This shows that Keisha is not head-over-heels in love with Andy and is not as involved in the relationship as Andy.

6. Tyrone's statement to the police after the accident included many details about that evening. In five sentences or less, summarize the most important facts Tyrone gives the police.
   All of the boys had been drinking that night except B.J. The car was swerving and people were honking to signal the car was weaving, but the boys thought it was funny. All of a sudden they hit a wall and Tyrone rolled out of the rear passenger door. He helped Andy out of the front seat and met B.J. by the front passenger seat where Rob was pinned in the car since he had his feet on the dashboard. They tried to get Rob out, but the engine caught fire and knocked the boys away from the car, while Rob screamed inside.

7. B.J. was the only one not drinking on the night of the accident. Later, he feels guilty and wonders if he should have stopped them from driving or offered to drive. What reason does he give for not speaking up?
   B.J. feels lucky to hang out with the other boys since he is not very popular and is the only one of the group not on the basketball team. He admits he is usually so happy to be invited out with the guys that he doesn't try to change what they are doing.

8. List the questions B.J. asks in his first prayer following the accident.
   B.J. asks why the accident happened, why Rob had to die, why he didn't die, how Robbie's mother is dealing with the accident, if it's his fault Robbie is dead, why he feels so guilty, if this was done to teach kids a lesson, and if this will stop others from drinking and driving.

9. What is Rhonda's most frightening moment?
   Rhonda's most frightening moment is realizing that young people can die.

10. What articles are in the *Herald*'s special edition? List their titles and write one sentence telling what each was about.
    In Memorium: Brief memorial to Robbie
    Canned Food Drive Begins: Asking students to be aware of those less fortunate and donate 5 canned goods
    International Guests: Students from West Africa visited the school and are interviewed about the experience
    Bus Changes: Warning students to control their behavior on the bus
    Editorial Comments: Looking at the accident from a "will kids ever learn" standpoint
    On Giving Thanks: Appreciating things students have that they take for granted
    Sports Scene: The basketball team forfeited two games and Andy was named the new captain
    Ski Trip All Downhill: Summary of ski trip
    Teacher of the Week: Coach Ripley of the basketball team sponsors the S.A.D.D. club and is respected by students

11. What are three points Andy makes when he talks to the coach on his first day back to school after the accident?
    Andy confesses he is hurting and having a difficult time dealing with the accident. He confesses he wished he had died right after the accident and wished it could have been him instead of Rob since Rob had so much going for him in life. He talks about how long he and Rob had been friends and how close they were, how he knew better than to drink and drive, how he was embarrassed for crying in court, and how he feels as though he should have received a tougher punishment in court.

Assignment 2
Sad Songs, Juicy Gossip-Ferocious Frustration

1. Rhonda mentions that grief counselors have come to the school to help students deal with the accident. What does she say really helps students the most in dealing with Rob's death?
   Rhonda says talking in small groups with students and teachers is what really helps the students deal with the death of their friend.

2. What three things would Gerald get rid of if he could change the world? Tell why he would get rid of each.
   Gerald says he would get rid of peanut butter, Band-Aids, and five dollar bills. These things are respectively symbolic of abandonment, prejudice, and abuse.

3. How does Andy's personality change following the accident? What do his friends begin to notice about him?
   Andy likes to be alone a lot, and he has crying spells. They also say he is depressed.

4. Who takes Rob's old position on the basketball court as center?
   Andy takes over Rob's position and is also the new team captain.
5. Andy is outstanding in the first basketball game after the accident. After the game, Coach tells Andy, "Without you, we'd fall apart." What is Andy's response?
   Andy admits that he isn't holding himself together and is still struggling to understand his feelings regarding the accident.
6. Rob's parents attend the first game after the accident. What effect does this have on the team and on Andy?
   The team plays better knowing that Rob's parents are in the stands. The presence of Rob's parents and the lack of Andy's parents makes Andy feel even more guilty that he lived instead of Rob.
7. How does Andy describe his relationship with his family to his psychologist?
   Andy says his parents don't understand him at all. His father works all the time and his mother is out of touch with reality. Andy feels like they love his younger brother more than him.
8. What is Keisha's response when Andy invites her to ride on the bus with him out to the mall to see a movie? Why is this response significant?
   Keisha tells Andy she is too busy with helping out at home and getting her school work done. This upsets Andy and makes him feel rejected by Keisha. It also shows that Keisha is beginning to lose her patience with Andy's outbursts.
9. Why does Andy choose to let his grades slide?
   Andy gives several reasons why he lets his grades slide. He says his parents push him to be something he isn't, his friends make fun of him if he does well, his counselor doesn't believe he will be able to be anything but an athlete, and his teachers set very low expectations for black students.

Assignment 3
Female Frustration-Black on White

1. Why does Keisha call her mother to come pick her and Andy up at the mall? *Keisha and Andy are having a good time until Andy sees the Santa display, which reminds him of Rob. All of a sudden he gets really depressed and stops talking. Keisha calls her mom to come pick them up when the day stops being fun for her and she gets bored.*
2. The December 20th assignments give us important information about each character and touch on many themes in the novel. What are the last two lines of each person's poem?
   Andy: "But the present is so heavy/ I don't think I'm going to last."
   Rhonda: "I've found the place/ where I belong."
   Keisha: "That you got a secret/ And it's going to blow."
   B.J.: "Just a sweet little lady/ That warms to my touch."
   Gerald: "I did my best with poetry/ But I just couldn't write it."
3. Andy tells his psychologist about being the victim of black stereotyping while shopping at the mall. What does he say used to happen when he and Rob would go shopping? *Andy says the salespeople in expensive stores would always follow him and Rob around, afraid they were going to steal. He also says they thought they were drug dealers and were using drug money to buy stuff other black people normally couldn't afford.*

4. When Dr. Carrothers asks Andy how his trip to the mall with Keisha went, what is Andy's response?
   Andy admits he got depressed while at the mall, but continues to say how great Keisha is and how she is very understanding and supportive when he gets down. He says their relationship is great, and she is the only one who helps him sort through his problems.

5. Andy tells Dr. Carrothers that Keisha is there for him when no one else is. What examples does he give to show that she is "there for him"?
   Keisha came to the hospital, the funeral, and the trial to support Andy. She is also the only person he feels like he can cry in front of, and when he does, she comforts him. Andy says he can always call her, and she will cheer him up.

6. Why doesn't Rob's mother mention "the rock" when she calls Andy on Christmas day?
   Rob's mother used to always tell Andy he could come over and pick up his rock, since bad kids always get rocks from Santa. Andy would always say he was good that year and then she would give him a present. When she calls the Christmas after Rob's death, she doesn't mention the rock because neither one would know how to handle the issue of whether or not Andy had been good this year.

7. Ms. Blackwell reads the poem "One Thousand Nine Hundred Sixty-Eight Winters" to the class. What is each student's response to the poem? Include responses by Andy, Gerald, Mary Alice, and Keisha.
   Andy: Finds the poem humorous and says he felt the exact same way that morning Gerald: Feels this way everyday, like there is always white smothering him all the time Mary Alice: Has trouble understanding Gerald's point of view, but then admits she's never really thought about it and concedes it probably is overwhelming Keisha: Agrees everyone feels like they stand out when they just want to blend in at some point, whether due to race or gender

8. When Andy tells Keisha he is being driven crazy by the thought of Robbie being cold out in the cemetery, what is Keisha's response?
   Keisha tells Andy he is driving her crazy and that Robbie can't feel anything. She then tells Andy that Robbie is warm and at peace to try to comfort him.

Assignment 4
Accepting Fear-The Importance of Friendship

1. What did Andy do when he and Keisha took a walk out to the freeway, and what was Keisha's response?
   Andy looks down over the railing and seriously considers jumping into the traffic to commit suicide. Keisha grabs him and demands he take her home, never mentioning what he almost did again.

2. What promise does Dr. Carrothers make Andy agree to during their therapy session?
   Dr. Carrothers makes Andy promise that if he ever gets too depressed he will call him before he tries to hurt himself.

3. What does Andy tell Keisha he sees in his future?
   Andy tells Keisha that he sees nothing in his future, all he sees is darkness and he doesn't see himself anywhere doing anything.

4. What does Rob tell Andy in the dream Andy has?
   Rob tells Andy to die so he can hang out with him in heaven. He also tells him the whole accident was his fault since he was driving and he bought the beer.

5. What does Andy say in his letter to Rob's parents?
   Andy asks for forgiveness, but says he understands if they cannot give it. He then makes a list of all the good things he remembers about Rob to help Rob's parents focus on the good memories instead of the bad reality.

6. When B.J. and Tyrone are concerned about Andy and go to talk to the school counselor about him, what is her response to their concerns?
   She tells the boys Andy is getting counseling outside of school and not to worry, he's getting the help he needs.

7. What does Andy tell Dr. Carrothers about Rob's dad's response to the letter? *Andy says Rob's dad has forgiven him but is having a harder time dealing with the situation than his mom, who is totally forgiving. Andy finds it easier to relate to how Rob's dad is feeling since he too is still wrestling with forgiveness and emotional issues from the accident.*

8. What does Andy say to Dr. Carrothers to convince the doctor that he has improved enough to have appointments on an as-needed basis?
   Andy says he's sleeping better and doing better in school. He admits he still blames himself but also says he is learning to live with the guilt. He says he has his act together and no longer needs to come to therapy.

9. What main points does Keisha make in her homework essay about the importance of friendship?
   Keisha says friends make life exciting and without them life would be boring and meaningless. She also says life without friends is very lonely since there is no one to share your thoughts with when you need to talk.

10. What is B.J.'s summary of *Macbeth*, and what is Andy's reaction to it?
    B.J. summarizes Macbeth *by saying the message is that life is short and then you die. He also says Macbeth thinks life doesn't mean anything, but believes this is only because he was the cause of so much death and couldn't find anything in life to be happy about. After hearing this Andy gets out of his seat and leaves the room suddenly.*

Assignment 5
Concern and Denial-Slipping Away

1. When Andy's teacher calls home to alert his parents that Andy could be in real trouble, what is Andy's father's response?
   Andy's father makes excuses for Andy and dismisses the idea that there is a problem. He tells Andy's teacher she is overly concerned about a situation that is under control.

2. Why does Monty put tears on his tiger?
   Monty puts tears on his tiger because his tiger is very sad, like Andy gets sometimes.

3. In the conversation between two teachers on February 25th, one teacher raises concerns about Andy and asks, "How could he be stable after only three months?" What is the second teacher's response?
   The second teacher doesn't think the accident affected him very much since black kids are "tough" after experiencing so much while growing up.

4. In her diary entry on March 9th, Keisha says Andy has his parents, teachers, and counselor all fooled into thinking he is adjusting well. According to Keisha, who is the only person who knows how troubled Andy really is?
    Keisha is the only one who really knows that Andy is in trouble.
5. What happens during the talent show when Andy tells Keisha that she sometimes gets on his nerves?
    Keisha says Andy gets on her nerves all the time, which leads to an exchange of rude comments and ultimately ends with Keisha breaking up with Andy.
6. Andy talks to his mother after the talent show, to try to explain to her how he feels. To what does he compare his feelings?
    Andy tells her a story of when he was nine and fell into a tide pool late at night. He was under water and couldn't breathe, and he was crying for help but it only made things worse. Andy tries to tell her that's how he feels now and that he can't handle this all by himself.
7. How does Andy's mother respond when Andy asks for help handling the accident?
    She tells him that time will heal all wounds and that he's young and resilient so he will bounce back.
8. After finding out he missed his opportunity with the basketball scouts, to what conclusion does Andy come?
    Andy decides he doesn't need college, basketball, Keisha, or anything at all. He has given up all hope on everything.
9. Describe Rhonda and Tyrone's relationship.
    Rhonda and Tyrone are in a happy relationship where Rhonda feels sparks each time she is with Tyrone. They have fun whenever they hang out and are in love with each other.
10. Rhonda tells Saundra all about Keisha and Andy's breaking up. What is Rhonda's final comment before going on to talk about her prom dress? *She says, "that dude needs help."*

Assignment 6
<u>A Father's Dream-End of Novel</u>
1. When Andy's father threatens to punish his son if he doesn't get his grades up, how does Andy respond?
    Andy tells his father there's no way to hurt him since he deals with hurt every day.
2. Why does Andy's father always call him "Andrew"?
    He wants Andy to have a name that will help him assimilate into the business world, one that will help him find success and be suitable for a special young man.
3. Which three people does Andy try to call before he kills himself, and what response does he get from each?
    Andy calls Dr. Carrothers, who is out of town and cannot take the call, Keisha, whose mother answers and says she is asleep, and his basketball coach, who is not home.
4. Why does Andy think tigers have it rough?
    Andy feels bad that tigers are stuck in cages at zoos and have no freedom. He says that tigers in zoos think they are equal to all the other tigers in the jungle, but they quickly learn they have to stay in their place and have no way out.

5. How does Andy kill himself?
   Andy shoots himself in the head with his father's shotgun.
6. What does Monty see on the ceiling?
   Andy's little brother Monty notices blood on the ceiling when he and his mother get home.
7. Why is Tyrone mad at the suicide prevention/grief counseling woman at their school?

   Tyrone is angry because he and B.J. went to the school counselor with their concerns about Andy and his depression, but no one did anything until it was too late. He wonders where the suicide posters and hotline numbers were last week when Andy was about to kill himself.
8. What does the grief counselor suggest Andy's friends should do to try to work through their pain and frustration over Andy's death?
   She recommends they each write a letter to Andy explaining how they feel.

9. How do each of Andy's friends react to his suicide?
   Tyrone: Says he will never understand why Andy did it and thinks Andy should have valued life more; very angry at Andy for what he did Gerald: Is very mad at Andy and says he was a coward; says he hates Andy for doing this
   Marcus: Says he always wanted to be like Andy but feels better about who he is since he never knew the pain Andy was going through
   Rhonda: Is mad Andy didn't think about his family or friends finding his body or dealing with his suicide
   Keisha: Shocked that Andy is actually dead and is upset that she has to stay behind and deal with the pain he caused
   B.J.: Prays to God to watch over Andy and help him find peace
10. What does Monty say he will never forget?
    Monty says he'll never forget that it's okay to put tears on a tiger.
11. When Monty goes to visit Andy's grave, he tells Andy how things have changed since he went away. How has the family changed?
    Andy's parents got a divorce and moved to new houses. Monty says they pay a lot of attention to him now that Andy is gone.

MULTIPLE CHOICE STUDY/QUIZ QUESTIONS
Tears of a Tiger

Assignment 1
Crash, Fire, Pain- "Hey, Coach! Can We Talk?"

1. According to the newspaper account, what happened on the evening of November 8th?

    A. Robbie Washington was walking home along the side of a dark road. Andy and two other boys had been drinking, and as they swerved to miss a deer, their car struck and killed Robbie.

    B. Andy Jackson was driving drunk while three friends rode with him in the car. There was an accident. Two of the friends were not injured, but one was trapped in the car and killed by the engine fire.

    C. Four friends left the basketball game and went to a nearby park. They had been drinking and picked a fight with some older guys. One of the guys pulled a knife and stabbed Robbie in the stomach, ultimately leading to his death.

    D. Andy was trying to drive his three friends home after the basketball game. The other three boys had been drinking and kept grabbing the steering wheel to make Andy lose control. The car ended up hitting a fence--injuring two boys and killing Robbie.

2. Describe the relationship between Andy and Rob as shown in their conversation after the basketball game on November 7th.

    A. Rob and Andy are step-brothers. They have some friendly rivalry between them, but that is usually because they are both competing for their mother's attention.

    B. Rob and Andy are jealous of each other. In the short conversation in the locker room it is obvious that Rob wishes he could play basketball at the same level as Andy. At the same time, Andy is jealous that Rob has a girlfriend while he is all alone.

    C. It is clear that Rob and Andy are not close friends. They make several mean comments back and forth after the game. It also seems Rob is trying to steal Andy's girlfriend, Keisha.

    D. It is clear that Rob and Andy are close friends through their friendly teasing back and forth. The two play off of each other well in boasting about the game, and they discuss a variety of issues, such as grades, parents, and girls in their short conversation.

3. Describe the relationship between Andy and Keisha based on Andy's comments after the game on November 7th.
    A. Andy is in control of his relationship with Keisha since he tells her what to do and she quickly obeys, showing that she is more in love with him then he is with her.
    B. Andy is torn between wanting to be with Keisha, who has been his best friend since elementary school, and wanting to be with Amanda, a new girl at school who is quickly becoming very popular.
    C. Though Andy is bragging about his relationship with Keisha, it is obvious from the teasing of the other boys that Keisha has the upper hand in the relationship and is very important to Andy.
    D. Though Keisha comes to the basketball game, it is clear that she is interested in someone else, even though Andy seems very interested in her.

4. Why doesn't Gerald go riding with his friends after the game?
    A. Gerald hints that his father is strict and says he must hurry home after the game to avoid a more serious situation.
    B. Gerald has been chasing after Rhonda for several months and she finally agreed to get pizza with him after the game.
    C. Gerald doesn't really like the other boys and worries that if he hangs out with them, he will get into trouble.
    D. Gerald's mother is very sick and needs his care almost full time so he hurries home to be with her.

5. How does Keisha respond to the news about the accident and Rob's death in her phone conversation with Rhonda?
    A. Keisha is worried only about Andy and whether he is okay. She is relieved to discover Rob is the only one who died and calls Rhonda to share her relief. She is very concerned Andy will not be able to deal with such an emotional tragedy.
    B. Keisha cannot handle the news of Rob's death and Andy's injuries. When she arrives at the hospital she passes out when hearing the news. When she finally gets to see Andy later that day, she stays with him for less than a minute because she cannot handle seeing him hurt.
    C. Keisha is worried about all four of the boys and hopes they are all okay. When she discovers Rob died, she has a hard time dealing with the news and tells Rhonda she's never known anyone who has died before, except her grandmother who was old.
    D. Keisha is worried about all four of the boys and hopes they are all okay. After hearing of Rob's death, she is relieved it was only him and not Andy. She tells Rhonda she wants to stay with Andy at the hospital all night and stay with him at home until he can return to school.

6. Tyrone's statement to the police after the accident included many details about that evening. In five sentences or less, summarize the most important facts Tyrone gives the police.

   A. All of the boys had been drinking that night except B.J. The car was swerving and people were honking to signal the car was weaving, but the boys thought it was funny. All of a sudden they hit a wall and Tyrone rolled out of the rear passenger door. He helped Andy out of the front seat and met B.J. by the front passenger seat where Rob was pinned in the car since he had his feet on the dashboard. They tried to get Rob out, but the engine fire made it impossible.

   B. Andy and the other boys had been drinking after the game. When Andy realized how late it was, he decided to get everyone home fast so he could get to Keisha's house. He was driving so fast that he couldn't avoid hitting a deer in the road. Tyrone, Andy, and B.J. got out safely, but the deer hit on Rob's side, and he was killed upon impact.

   C. B.J. begged Andy and the others to let him drive that night since he was the only one not drinking. The other boys laughed at him and called him short, making him upset. As they were driving, B.J. kicked Andy from the backseat, unintentionally forcing Andy to lose control of the car, hitting a tree. Tyrone pulled Andy out of the car and went to help B.J. try to rescue Rob, who was pinned in the vehicle, but they were unable to do so before he died.

   D. Andy and Rob had been drinking that night and made a bet that Andy could steer the car with his feet. As Andy was using his feet to steer, he lost control and slammed into another car. The car flipped over several times and pinned both Andy and Rob in the car. Tyrone and B.J. got out and pulled Andy out of the car. When they got to Rob, he had already died.

7. B.J. was the only one not drinking on the night of the accident. Later, he feels guilty and wonders if he should have stopped them from driving or offered to drive. What reason does he give for not speaking up?

   A. He has tried to stop them before but knows they never listen.

   B. He feels lucky to hang out with them, so he never tries to change their plans.

   C. He worries they will get angry and leave him on the side of the road.

   D. He knows the guys would have made fun of him.

8. What types of questions does B.J. ask in his prayer following the accident?

   A. He asks questions that deal with how it will feel to be at the funeral and whether or not Andy will have to go to jail.

   B. He asks questions that deal with why the accident happened and whether or not he is to blame.

   C. He asks questions that deal with death in general and whether or not he will ever be able to stop reliving the events each night as he sleeps.

   D. He asks questions that deal with how Andy is going to recover and whether or not they can still be friends.

9. What is Rhonda's most frightening moment?
   A. Realizing that young people can die
   B. Learning that death is hard to overcome
   C. Thinking that maybe is was all four of the boys who had died
   D. Watching as Rob's body is lowered into the ground

10. Which is NOT the topic of an article in the *Herald* after the accident?
    A. An article asking students to be aware of those who are less fortunate and to donate canned goods
    B. An article about Coach Ripley
    C. An article warning students to control their behavior on the bus
    D. An article about ways to deal with death and loss of a loved one, including hotline numbers students could call for help

11. What are three points Andy makes when he talks to the coach on his first day back to school after the accident?
    A. Andy says he is handling the accident just fine and is just wishing his life would get back to normal. He says he misses his friend but has realized there is nothing he could have done to save him. He also feels he was treated fairly in court.
    B. Andy says he has really relied on the support of his friends and family in the last few days. He thinks that Rob would have forgiven him for what happened. He also says he is fighting the court sentence he received since it was an accident but the judge sentenced him as if he did it intentionally.
    C. Andy confesses he is having a difficult time dealing with the accident. He says he wished he had died right after the accident and wished it could have been him instead of Rob. He also feels as if he should have been punished more by the court.
    D. Andy confesses he tried to commit suicide in the days following the accident. He says his parents blame him and Rob's parents yelled at him about killing their only son. He also says that he is not planning on following through with his court sentence because they cannot punish him any more than he is punishing himself.

Assignment 2
Sad Songs, Juicy Gossip-Ferocious Frustration

1. Rhonda mentions that grief counselors have come to the school to help students deal with the accident. What does she say really helps students the most in dealing with Rob's death?
    A. Talking in small groups with other students
    B. Writing a letter to Rob's parents
    C. Talking one-on-one with a counselor
    D. Writing a poem about their emotions

2. What three things would Gerald get rid of if he could change the world? Tell why he would get rid of each.
    A. Gerald says he would get rid of peanut butter, Band-Aids, and five dollar bills. These things are symbolic of abandonment, prejudice, and abuse.
    B. Gerald says he would get rid of ice, the color blue, and clocks. All of these things attribute to his inability to fit in with the other students at his school due to his drastically different social background.
    C. Gerald says he would get rid of basketball nets, combs, and shoe laces. These things are symbolic of racism, ignorance, and control.
    D. Gerald says he would get rid of beer, windshields, and interstate walls. These things all attributed to the death of Rob and the emotional problems his three other friends have.

3. How does Andy's personality change following the accident? What do his friends begin to notice about him?
    A. Andy likes to be alone a lot, and he has crying spells. They also say he is depressed.
    B. Andy hates hanging out with any of his old friends and tries to avoid them at all costs. They all say he has become mean.
    C. Andy never makes eye contact and has become quiet. They also say he seems more violent.
    D. Andy has become very outgoing and loud. They all noticed he seems to be trying to hide something.

4. Who takes Rob's old position on the basketball court as center?
    A. Gerald
    B. Tyrone
    C. Andy
    D. Kevin

5. Andy is outstanding in the first basketball game after the accident. After the game, Coach tells Andy, "Without you, we'd fall apart." What is Andy's response?

   A. He smiles and asks his coach if he thinks he will be able to get a college scholarship to make Rob proud.

   B. He stays quiet and doesn't respond to his coach since he can't find the words to explain how guilty he feels.

   C. He gets choked up and begins to cry because he knows it should be Rob holding the team together, not him.

   D. He admits that he isn't holding himself together and is still struggling to understand his feelings regarding the accident.

6. Rob's parents attend the first game after the accident. What effect does this have on the team and on Andy?

   A. The team has trouble focusing on the game with Rob's parents there. Andy feels more confident since it appears as though they have really forgiven him, and he plays much better because of this.

   B. The team is moved by their presence and encouraged to play their best. Andy is bothered by Rob's parents' being at the game and has to step out for a few minutes to regain his composure.

   C. The guys on the team don't notice Rob's parents in the stands. Andy sees them and is honored they came to the game. This also makes him wish he were their son since they are so supportive and encouraging.

   D. The team plays better knowing that Rob's parents are in the stands. The presence of Rob's parents and the lack of Andy's parents makes Andy feel even more guilty that he lived instead of Rob.

7. How does Andy describe his relationship with his family to his psychologist?

   A. He says his parents are like any other parents. His father gets on his case from time to time, and his mother is very involved in his life. He just feels like any other average teenager with a normal family life.

   B. He says his parents don't understand him at all. His father works all the time and his mother is out of touch with reality. He feels like they love his younger brother more than him.

   C. He says his parents fight all the time and make life hard for him and his brother. His father drinks and takes it out on the family, making his mother depressed. He feels like his home life is tough.

   D. He says his parents are hard on him sometimes, but he knows it's because they love him. His father wants him to go to college and his mother encourages him to do his best in everything. He sometimes feels annoyed and pressured but ultimately knows they love him.

8. What is Keisha's response when Andy invites her to ride on the bus with him out to the mall to see a movie? Why is this response significant?

   A. Keisha looks surprised and doesn't know what to say. She thought he had forgotten about her, showing that there are growing problems in their relationship.

   B. Keisha tells Andy she already has plans with Rhonda. This hurts Andy; it shows that Keisha is losing interest in him and would rather spend her time with someone else.

   C. Keisha tells Andy she is too busy. This upsets Andy and makes him feel rejected by Keisha. It also shows that Keisha is beginning to lose her patience with Andy's outbursts.

   D. Keisha wraps her arms around Andy and kisses him with excitement. This shows that Andy is finally acting more like himself and moving on after the accident.

9. Why does Andy choose to let his grades slide?

   A. He says his parents push him to be something he isn't, his friends make fun of him if he does well, and his teachers set very low expectations for black students like him.

   B. He says his teachers make fun of him, his friends have abandoned him after the accident, and his parents are never home to help him when he needs it.

   C. He says he already has rejection letters from four colleges, he has no money for college, and he has too much to deal with from the accident.

   D. He says he can't focus on his school work because all he can think about is Rob, and no one understands what he is going through.

Assignment 3
Female Frustration-Black on White

1. Why does Keisha call her mother to come pick her and Andy up at the mall?

    A. Andy is being loud in the department store, and the sales woman asks him to leave. He makes a big scene, and when security arrives they take Keisha and Andy into custody until an adult picks them up.

    B. Andy wants to buy Keisha a present but doesn't want her to know what it is. He tells Keisha to have her mom pick her up so he could buy her a gift.

    C. Andy gets really depressed and stops talking. She calls her mom to come pick them up when the day stops being fun for her and she gets bored with Andy's mood.

    D. Andy and Keisha run into B.J. and Tyrone in the food court. Andy starts horsing around with his friends and ignores Keisha, so she calls her mom to pick her up.

2. The December 20th poetry assignments give us important information about each character and touch on many themes in the novel. Below, each character's name is next to the last two lines of his/her poem. Which one has the incorrect lines next to it?

    A. Rhonda: I've found the place/ Where I belong

    B. B.J.: Just a sweet little lady/ That warms to my touch

    C. Andy: The past was a fright/ But the future looks bright

    D. Keisha: That you got a secret/ And it's going to blow

3. Andy tells his psychologist about being the victim of black stereotyping while shopping at the mall. What does he say used to happen when he and Rob would go shopping?

    A. Andy says the salespeople in expensive stores laugh at the boys when they want to look at nice items. They come right out and say that there is no way poor kids like them have money to buy nice things, and they tell them to stop wasting their time.

    B. Andy says the salespeople in expensive stores would always follow him and Rob around, afraid they were going to steal. He also says they thought they were drug dealers and were using drug money to buy stuff other black people normally couldn't afford.

    C. Andy says they are completely ignored as they shop in nice store. If they ask to try something on, the sales people act like they don't exist and wait on their white customers first. They only way they get attention is on the way out when the salespeople are worried that the boys stole something.

    D. Andy says mall security follows them around in each store they go into. He says they often ask to search the boys before they leave the store, assuming they stole something. He also says store clerks refuse to help them when they want to buy something.

4. When Dr. Carrothers asks Andy how his trip to the mall with Keisha went, what is Andy's response?
   A. He says he had a great time and really felt like the mall helped create a real Christmas spirit within him, pulling him out of the depression he has been in.
   B. He admits he got in trouble but says it was no big deal and that his parents never found out.
   C. He says he made Keisha mad and they fought about it later, but they are in love-- and she always forgives him no matter how many mistakes he makes.
   D. Andy admits he got depressed, but says how great Keisha is and how she is very understanding and supportive when he gets "down."

5. Andy tells Dr. Carrothers that Keisha is there for him when no one else is. What examples does he give to show that she is "there for him"?
   A. She encourages him to write out his feelings in a journal and then talk about them with others. He also says that she is the only person who understands how important therapy is.
   B. She came to the hospital, the funeral, and the trial. She is the only person he can cry in front of, and when he does, she comforts him. He also says when he calls her she cheers him up.
   C. She goes to the cemetery with him each week to put fresh flowers on Robbie's grave. He also says she is the only one who listens to him.
   D. She comes over to his house every day so he doesn't have to be alone with his dark thoughts. He also says that she helps keep him organized and prepared for his classes at school.

6. Why doesn't Rob's mother mention "the rock" when she calls Andy on Christmas Day?
   A. Neither one would know how to handle the issue of whether or not Andy had been good this year.
   B. Neither one wanted to think about God after He had just taken Robbie's life.
   C. Neither one wanted to have to go to the park together to find a rock for that year.
   D. Neither one could handle the idea of Robbie's not getting to be part of the tradition.

7. Ms. Blackwell reads the poem "One Thousand Nine Hundred Sixty-Eight Winters" to the class. What is each student's response to the poem? Include responses by Andy, Gerald, Mary Alice, and Keisha.

   A. Andy and Gerald think the poem is funny and neglect to take any real meaning from it. Mary Alice and Keisha are more mature and understand the point the author is trying to make and feel like it applies to their lives in many ways.

   B. Andy and Keisha think the poem is inappropriate for school and are shocked the teacher read it to the class. Gerald, being the smartest in the class, really understands it and can see past the literal meaning, while Mary Alice is offended and leaves class.

   C. Andy is deeply disturbed by the author's words and begins to cry. Gerald and Keisha are moved by the poem as well, but look at it from an opposite view of Andy, making some valid points. Mary Alice understands the poem but doesn't make a personal connection with it like the other students.

   D. Andy thinks the poem is funny and can relate to it. Gerald and Keisha truly understand the meaning and say they feel the same way the author describes. Mary Alice doesn't really appreciate the meaning, but acknowledges she's never really thought about it before.

8. When Andy tells Keisha he is being driven crazy by the thought of Robbie being cold out in the cemetery, what is Keisha's response?

   A. She is moved by his sadness and cries.

   B. She laughs at Andy and says he is stupid.

   C. She takes him to church to get help.

   D. She tells Andy he is driving her crazy.

Assignment 4
Accepting Fear-The Importance of Friendship

1. What does Andy do when he and Keisha take a walk out to the freeway, and what is Keisha's response?

    A. Andy looks down over the railing and seriously considers jumping into the traffic to commit suicide. Keisha grabs him and demands for him to take her home, never again mentioning what he almost did.

    B. Andy puts flowers and a small plaque at the accident site as a memorial to Robbie. Keisha begins to cry and tells Andy that they have to move on and stop thinking about Rob's death so much.

    C. Andy throws an empty beer bottle over the railing and nearly hits a car. Keisha tries to pull Andy away, but all he can do is say how meaningless life is and look for more trash to throw at oncoming cars.

    D. Andy punches the wall in the same place their car hit, nearly breaking his hand on the hard cement. Keisha yells at him to calm down and then convinces him to leave the accident site.

2. What promise does Dr. Carrothers make Andy agree to during their therapy session?

    A. That Andy will continue to stay in contact with Rob's parents until he sorts through all of his emotions

    B. That if Andy ever gets too depressed, he will call Dr. Carrothers before he tries to hurt himself

    C. That Andy will try to communicate with his father at least once a day and will try to build a better relationship with him

    D. That when Andy graduates from high school, he will pick a career that will help people instead of one that will make him a lot of money

3. What does Andy tell Keisha he sees in his future?
    A. Children
    B. Nothing
    C. College
    D. Marriage

4. What does Rob tell Andy in the dream Andy has?
    A. To always remember him no matter what
    B. To forgive himself because the accident wasn't his fault
    C. To die so he can hang out with him in heaven
    D. To move on with his life and be happy

5. What does Andy say in his letter to Rob's parents?
    A. He asks for forgiveness and makes a list of all the good things he remembers about Rob.
    B. He tells them he is considering suicide and admits it wasn't even his idea to help Rob.
    C. He admits he bought the beer and includes a photo of Rob from earlier that night.
    D. He tells them he is sorry and writes a short poem remembering Rob.

6. When B.J. and Tyrone are concerned about Andy and go to talk to the school counselor about him, what is her response to their concerns?
    A. Andy is getting counseling outside of school and not to worry, he's getting the help he needs.
    B. They should just give Andy his space and let him grieve in any way he needs.
    C. They should talk to Andy and try to work through their problems together since they were all involved in the accident.
    D. Andy is in high school and needs to learn how to deal with his own problems, so let him work it out on his own.

7. What does Andy tell Dr. Carrothers about Rob's dad's response to the letter?
    A. He says Rob's dad refused to read the letter, saying it would be too painful.
    B. He says Rob's dad hugged him and thanked him for the letter, saying it meant a lot to him.
    C. He says Rob's dad is unable to forgive him for killing his son.
    D. He says Rob's dad has forgiven him but is having a harder time dealing with his emotions.

8. What does Andy say to Dr. Carrothers to convince the doctor that he has improved enough to have appointments on an as-needed basis?
    A. He says he has improved his relationship with his parents and feels like he can talk to them now. He says he doesn't need a therapist because his parents can help him.
    B. He says his has stopped thinking about suicide and is a happier person. He says he has forgiven himself and no longer feels guilty.
    C. He says his parents can no longer afford private therapy, and he will just talk with the school counselor unless things get bad again.
    D. He says he's sleeping better and doing better in school. He admits he still blames himself but says that he is learning to live with the guilt.

9. What main points does Keisha make in her homework essay about the importance of friendship?

   A. She says friends are disappointing and let you down. She says Andy has let her down by not listening to her problems, and she's upset with where their relationship is headed.

   B. She says friends are not always the most reliable people. She says friends tend to forget about you when they get a boyfriend and are never around anymore.

   C. She says her friendship with Andy is the most important friendship she's ever had. She also says she doesn't think she or Andy would have been able to survive this year without each other.

   D. She says friends make life exciting and without them life would be boring and meaningless. She also says life without friends is very lonely since there is no one to share your thoughts with when you need to talk.

10. What is B.J.'s summary of *Macbeth*, and what is Andy's reaction to it?

    A. He says life is about admitting your mistakes. He also says Macbeth is a coward because he doesn't admit that he did something wrong. After hearing this Andy gets out of his seat and leaves the room suddenly.

    B. He says life is short and then you die. He also says Macbeth thinks life doesn't mean anything, but believes this is only because he was the cause of so much death and couldn't find anything in life to be happy about. After hearing this Andy yells at B.J. and throws a desk, telling him he's judging him too hard.

    C. He says life is about admitting your mistakes. He also says Macbeth is a coward because he doesn't admit that he did something wrong. After hearing this Andy yells at B.J. and throws a desk, telling B.J. he's judging him too hard.

    D. He says life is short and then you die. He also says Macbeth thinks life doesn't mean anything, but believes this is only because he was the cause of so much death and couldn't find anything in life to be happy about. After hearing this Andy gets out of his seat and leaves the room suddenly.

Assignment 5
Concern and Denial-Slipping Away

1. When Andy's teacher calls home to alert his parents that Andy could be in real trouble, what is Andy's father's response?

    A. He is outraged that Andy is acting out at school and is noticeably angry on the phone. He tells Andy's teacher he will punish Andy immediately and to consider the problem solved.

    B. He is mad at the teacher for accusing Andy of such ridiculous behavior. He tells Andy's teacher she is racist, and he is going to speak to the principal about her.

    C. He is upset and confused and begins crying on the phone. He tells Andy's teacher he has no way of helping Andy and doesn't know what to do.

    D. He makes excuses for Andy and dismisses the idea that there is a problem. He tells Andy's teacher she is overly concerned about a situation that is under control.

2. Why does Monty put tears on his tiger?

    A. Because his tiger has no friends and was just dumped by his girlfriend, like Andy

    B. Because his tiger is very sad, like Andy gets sometimes

    C. Because his tiger was just in a bad accident, just like Andy

    D. Because his tiger is hurting very badly, like Andy is sometimes

3. In the conversation between two teachers on February 25th, one teacher raises concerns about Andy and asks, "How could he be stable after only three months?" What is the second teacher's response?

    A. She believes black kids deal with death better, making this easier on Andy.

    B. She thinks black people forget things really quickly, so Andy hardly ever thinks about it.

    C. She stereotypes all black kids as being tough, and says the accident probably didn't really bother Andy.

    D. She doesn't think black kids feel pain, so Andy couldn't really be hurting.

4. In her diary entry on March 9th, Keisha says Andy has his parents, teachers, and counselor all fooled into thinking he is adjusting well. According to Keisha, who is the only person who knows how troubled Andy really is?

    A. Keisha

    B. B.J.

    C. Tyrone

    D. Rhonda

5. What happens during the talent show when Andy tells Keisha that she sometimes gets on his nerves?

    A. Keisha cries and begs Andy to forgive her, promising to be a better girlfriend in the future.

    B. Keisha says Andy gets on her nerves all the time, and she breaks up with him.

    C. Keisha tells Andy she's pregnant, and she wants him to have nothing to do with her or the baby.

    D. Keisha pushes Andy, and he falls onto the stage very embarrassed in front of the whole school.

6. Andy talks to his mother after the talent show, to try to explain to her how he feels. To what does he compare his feelings?

    A. A coma

    B. Numbness

    C. Death

    D. Drowning

7. How does Andy's mother respond when Andy asks for help handling the accident?

    A. She tells him it's all her fault and that she should have realized he needed help sooner.

    B. She tells him she will do everything she can to help him, including coming home earlier to spend more time with him.

    C. She tells him that time will heal all wounds and that he's young and resilient so he will bounce back.

    D. She tells him she doesn't know any way to help him and that he should talk to his dad.

8. After finding out he missed his opportunity with the basketball scouts, to what conclusion does Andy come?

    A. He doesn't need school or sports and will just drop out and get a job.

    B. He doesn't need college, basketball, Keisha, or anything at all. He has given up all hope on everything.

    C. He will work really hard the next few games to catch their attention once again and get the scholarship.

    D. He will give up on sports but focus on improving his grades so he can go to college to become a lawyer.

9. Describe Rhonda and Tyrone's relationship.

   A. They are in a happy relationship where Rhonda feels sparks each time she is with Tyrone. They have fun whenever they hang out and are in love with each other.

   B. They are in a dangerous relationship where Rhonda takes a lot of verbal abuse from Tyrone. They also take part in a lot of illegal activities that could land them in a lot of trouble.

   C. They are in an argumentative relationship. They tend to fight over little things, and it seems they go longer and longer without speaking.

   D. They are in an unrealistic relationship where Rhonda and Tyrone are pretending everything is okay when it really isn't. They both pretend to be happy, but really they are both wanting to break up.

10. Rhonda tells Saundra all about Keisha and Andy's breaking up. What is Rhonda's final comment before going on to talk about her prom dress?

    A. "I totally agree with Keisha."

    B. "I totally agree with Andy."

    C. "Now I can go out with Andy."

    D. "That dude needs help."

Assignment 6
A Father's Dream-End of Novel

1. When Andy's father threatens to punish his son if he doesn't get his grades up, how does Andy respond?

    A. Andy starts to shake and cry, telling his dad he's going to commit suicide.

    B. Andy tells his father there's no way to hurt him since he deals with hurt every day.

    C. Andy threatens to run away from home and never speak to his parents again.

    D. Andy punches the wall in the kitchen, making his father realize something is very wrong with his son.

2. Why does Andy's father always call him "Andrew"?

    A. He thinks Andrew is a powerful name since it means fortune and strength, so he uses it when he speaks to his son hoping the meaning of his name will have some affect on Andy's life.

    B. He had a friend in high school named Andy and didn't want to be reminded of him, so he always called him by his full name.

    C. He wanted people to think of Andrew Jackson when they heard his name since he was one of the most respectable presidents in the nation's history.

    D. He wants Andy to have a name that would help him assimilate into the business world, one that would help him find success, and one that would suit a special young man.

3. Which three people does Andy try to call before he kills himself, and what response does he get from each?

    A. He tries to talk to his mom, who is working on stuff for the homeowners' group, his dad, who is working late at the office, and his brother, who is too young to understand.

    B. He calls Rhonda, who is busy hanging out with Tyrone, Keisha, who is studying, and his coach, who is not at home.

    C. He calls Dr. Carrothers, who is out of town and cannot take the call, Keisha, whose mother answers and says she is asleep, and his basketball coach, who is not home.

    D. He calls Tyrone, who is out on a date with Rhonda, Keisha, who is still mad at him from the talent show, and B.J., who is at church.

4. Why does Andy think tigers have it rough?

    A. They are forced to endure the horrible conditions at the zoo.

    B. They have no freedom and learn they must stay in their place.

    C. They are bred for entertainment and fighting and nothing else.

    D. They have to live alone in the world without anyone for comfort or companionship.

5. How does Andy kill himself?
    A. He jumps off an overpass into heavy traffic.
    B. He slits his wrists and bleeds out in the bathroom.
    C. He shoots himself in the head with his father's shotgun.
    D. He overdoses on pain medication left over from the accident.

6. What does Monty see on the ceiling?
    A. A note
    B. A hole from the shotgun
    C. A noose
    D. Blood

7. Why is Tyrone mad at the suicide prevention/grief counseling woman at their school?
    A. He is angry because she is putting all the blame of Andy's suicide on the student body for not noticing his depression and trying to help.
    B. He is angry because he called the hotline, and no one ever contacted Andy to see if he was okay until two days after his suicide.
    C. He is angry because she doesn't know how to help the student body deal with Andy's suicide. All her suggestions don't seem to help anyone feel better about what happened.
    D. He is angry because he and B.J. went to the school counselor with their concerns about Andy and his depression, but no one did anything until it was too late.

8. What does the grief counselor suggest Andy's friends should do to try to work through their pain and frustration over Andy's death?
    A. Pray for help is dealing with the pain
    B. Write a letter to Andy explaining how they feel
    C. Attend a grief counseling seminar at the community outreach center
    D. Share their feelings one at a time while others listen

9. How do Andy's friends react to his suicide?
    A. They are all depressed and upset. Tyrone and B.J. even consider committing suicide themselves from having to deal with the pain.
    B. They are all stunned and don't know why it happened. Everyone at school thought Andy was completely happy.
    C. They are all very upset and angry. They have a difficult time understanding why he did it and feel like he took a coward's way out.
    D. They are not very surprised. Most students knew Andy was suffering and his suicide didn't come as much of a shock.

10. What does Monty say he will never forget?

   A. He'll never forget that when he grows up he will be a tiger like his brother.

   B. He'll never forget that it's okay to put tears on a tiger.

   C. He'll never forget that tigers have to die sometime.

   D. He'll never forget his brother was as strong as a tiger.

11. When Monty goes to visit Andy's grave, he tells Andy how things have changed since he went away. How has the family changed?

   A. Andy's parents throw themselves into their work to try to forget what happened. No one pays attention to Monty because it is too painful.

   B. Andy's parents are very depressed and are having a tough time coping. Monty gets a lot of attention now that Andy is gone, but he doesn't like it.

   C. Andy's parents get a divorce and move to new houses. Monty says they pay a lot of attention to him now that Andy is gone.

   D. Andy's parents are closer than ever and rely on each other for support. They are all in counseling as a family, and things are really improving.

ANSWER KEY: STUDY QUESTIONS *Tears of a Tiger*

	1	2	3	4	5	6
1	B	A	C	A	D	B
2	D	A	C	B	B	D
3	C	A	B	B	C	C
4	A	C	D	C	A	B
5	C	D	B	A	B	C
6	A	D	A	A	D	D
7	B	B	D	D	C	D
8	B	C	D	D	B	B
9	A	A		D	A	C
10	D			D	D	B

VOCABULARY WORKSHEETS

VOCABULARY ASSIGNMENT 1 *Tears of a Tiger*

Part I: Using Prior Knowledge and Contextual Clues

Below are the sentences in which the vocabulary words appear in the text. Read the sentence. Use any clues you can find in the sentence combined with your prior knowledge, and write what you think the underlined words mean on the lines provided.

1. No wonder you only scored six tonight. You too busy scopin' the women in the stands. Keisha got your nose wide open. She say "jump" and you say "how high." --Hey, jumpin' with Keisha is like touchin' the sky. I'd say I had an <u>honorable</u> excuse, my man.

   _____

2. Mama says the Lord knows all, and that He and His <u>infinite</u> wisdom knows the reason for all things.

   _____

3. Last week, a group of students from French West Africa visited Hazelwood as part of the International Exchange Experience. They visited Madame Loisel's advanced French classes and amazed the students with their <u>vast</u> knowledge of not only French, but also English, Swahili, and several African dialects.

   _____

4. Last week, a group of students from French West Africa visited Hazelwood as part of the International Exchange Experience. They visited Madame Loisel's advanced French classes and amazed the students with their vast knowledge of not only French, but also English, Swahili, and several African <u>dialects</u>.

   _____

5. Students who ride the yellow buses are reminded that fighting and other <u>undignified</u> behavior will result in a suspension from the bus and possible suspension from school.

   _____

6. Vice Principal Leo Davis has said that all incidents of disorderly conduct and <u>unruly</u> behavior must be eliminated in order to insure the safety of all concerned.

   _____

7. We are <u>accustomed</u> to whining about how small our allowances are, or how upset we are because we only have three pairs of athletic shoes, when there are so many around us who have *no* money, no homes, and no shoes at all.

   _____

Tears of a Tiger Vocabulary Worksheet Assignment 1 Continued

8. The team decided to forfeit the next two games and to dedicate the rest of the season to Rob and to try to win the title as a <u>tribute</u> to him.

_____

9. Well, except for the miscellaneous Band-Aids, I'd say you look pretty good, considering. Have you <u>recuperated</u> from that court ordeal yet?

_____

Part II: Determining the Meaning -- Match the vocabulary words to their dictionary definitions.

____ 1. HONORABLE   A. Returned to health or strength; recovered

____ 2. INFINITE   B. In the habit of; used to

____ 3. VAST   C. Lacking respect and honor

____ 4. DIALECT   D. A regional or social variety of a language distiguished by pronunciation, grammar, or vocabulary

____ 5. UNDIGNIFIED   E. An acknowledgment of gratitude, respect, or admiration

____ 6. UNRULY   F. Difficult or impossible to discipline or control

____ 7. ACCUSTOMED   G. Deserving or winning respect or distinction

____ 8. TRIBUTE   H. Very great in area or extent; immense

____ 9. RECUPERATED   I. Immeasurably great or large; boundless

VOCABULARY ASSIGNMENT 2 *Tears of a Tiger*

Part I: Using Prior Knowledge and Contextual Clues

Below are the sentences in which the vocabulary words appear in the text. Read the sentence. Use any clues you can find in the sentence combined with your prior knowledge, and write what you think the underlined words mean on the lines provided.

1. The Tigers really want to win this one because this is their first home game since that devastating loss of their popular and <u>capable</u> center, Robbie Washington.
   _____

2. The ball is passed now to Mills, to Shuttlesworth, and to Jackson who seems almost <u>frenzied</u> out there. He grabs the ball, gets up close, and *dunks* it in!
   _____

3. It's hard for us to understand why things like this happen, and I think you're doing a <u>remarkable</u> job of handling a very rough situation.
   _____

4. And I'm a psychologist, not a psychiatrist. . . . They make more money. No, just kidding. They can <u>dispense</u> medication, and I don't.
   _____

5. Do you know that she still says "Negro" and refuses to call us black or African-American? . . . She says her skin is *not* black and never will be and that she doesn't know anyone from Africa; why should she change what has worked perfectly well all her life? I've given up tryin' to <u>convert</u> her.
   _____

6. I'm not jealous, but I think they like him better. He's still cute and charmin' and hasn't started to get <u>rebellious</u> or misunderstood yet.
   _____

7. [Keisha] I wish I could, Andy, but I got a chemistry test tomorrow, plus I got to finish that composition for English class. . . . Then I told my mother that I'd start dinner. . . . [Andy] Be like that, then! See if I care! All I ask for is a little of your time, and you want to get all <u>righteous</u> on me. I'll go to the movies by myself!
   _____

8. If I remember, when I was in high school, the counselor was there to help kids out who had academic problems, or problems at home. . . . I just happened to be <u>fortunate</u> enough to find a lady who recognized a spark in me and gave me some direction.
   _____

Tears of a Tiger Vocabulary Worksheet Assignment 2 Continued

Part II: Determining the Meaning -- Match the vocabulary words to their dictionary definitions.

____ 1.   CAPABLE   A. Persuade to adopt a particular belief

____ 2.   FRENZIED   B. Worthy of notice or attention

____ 3.   REMARKABLE   C. Deal out; distribute

____ 4.   DISPENSE   D. Acting in an upright, moral way; virtuous

____ 5.   CONVERT   E. Going against control or authority

____ 6.   REBELLIOUS   F. Wildly excited or enthusiastic

____ 7.   RIGHTEOUS   G. Having ability

____ 8.   FORTUNATE   H. Lucky

VOCABULARY ASSIGNMENT 3 *Tears of a Tiger*

Part I: Using Prior Knowledge and Contextual Clues

Below are the sentences in which the vocabulary words appear in the text. Read the sentence. Use any clues you can find in the sentence combined with your prior knowledge, and write what you think the underlined words mean on the lines provided.

1. His smile can make me feel <u>desire</u>. His eyes are kind, his arms are strong, I've found the place where I belong.

   _____

2. She said listen to my music but *my* music makes good sense. 'Cause rappers speak in street talk and are never hard or <u>dense</u>.

   _____

3. My partner and I are interested in purchasing one of your more expensive <u>commodities</u>. Would you be so kind as to allow me to try on this leather coat?

   _____

4. I know they thought we were scopin' them for a robbery--if you look back into the store right after we left, you could see her writin' down <u>vital</u> information, scriblin' furiously our height and weight and skin color so she can identify us when we come back to rob her silly behind.

   _____

5. [Andy] And if you ain't got no money or no credit card, you can just pass up the Magic Midtowne Mall, 'cause we're takin' up a parkin' space from payin' customers. [Psychologist] Very <u>cynical</u> observation, but probably true.

   _____

6. Perhaps we need to discuss some <u>aspects</u> of your life just a little more. And once you get started, you don't really seem to mind, am I right?

   _____

7. I'm not sure, Andy, but it certainly is <u>apparent</u> in literature. I don't think it's completely racially motivated, however. The tones of black and white have the greatest amount of contrast between them, therefore writers and poets, who have always dealt with extremes in passion and people, use black and white to create those images of contrast.

   _____

8. As you have shown, color is used all the time to create images in our mind. It's society that <u>implants</u> positives and negatives onto certain ideas.

   _____

Tears of a Tiger Vocabulary Worksheet Assignment 3 Continued

Part II: Determining the Meaning -- Match the vocabulary words to their dictionary definitions.

____ 1. DESIRE   A. Easily perceived or understood

____ 2. DENSE   B. A longing for; wanting

____ 3. COMMODITIES   C. Of critical importance

____ 4. VITAL   D. Parts; features; phases

____ 5. CYNICAL   E. Distrusting or seeing the worst in the motives of others

____ 6. ASPECTS   F. Difficult to understand or follow because of being closely packed with ideas or complexities of style

____ 7. APPARENT   G. Sets securely in place

____ 8. IMPLANTS   H. Articles of trade or commerce; products

VOCABULARY ASSIGNMENT 4 *Tears of a Tiger*

Part I: Using Prior Knowledge and Contextual Clues
    Below are the sentences in which the vocabulary words appear in the text. Read the sentence. Use any clues you can find in the sentence combined with your prior knowledge, and write what you think the underlined words mean on the lines provided.

1. You're hurting and you can't find an escape from the pain and you're frightened because the only way out seems to be something you can't even verbalize. Am I right?

    _____

2. Sometimes it's part of the guilt and grieving process--to consider suicide as an alternative to the pain. But the answer is *life*, Andy, not death. So then I'd tell you about the other alternatives to help eliminate the pain.

    _____

3. Sometimes it's part of the guilt and grieving process--to consider suicide as an alternative to the pain. But the answer is *life*, Andy, not death. So then I'd tell you about the other alternatives to help eliminate the pain.

    _____

4. Sometimes it's part of the guilt and grieving process--to consider suicide as an alternative to the pain. But the answer is *life*, Andy, not death. So then I'd tell you about the other alternatives to help eliminate the pain.

    _____

5. Like how much fun you can be sometimes. Like how patient you are with Monty. Like how things brighten up when you're smiling.

    _____

6. He's got one little spark left--his refusal to surrender to Macduff and the forces of good--but don't you think his death is inevitable, Marcus? --Yeah, he deserves to die.

    _____

7. But Lady Macbeth, who seemed so strong at the beginning of the play, had a rather rapid mental deterioration--remember she was walking and talking in her sleep and washing her hands uncontrollably?

    _____

8. Well, I probably shouldn't tell you boys this, but he *is* getting some outside counseling. I tell you this in the strictest of confidences, because you seem to be so genuinely concerned. So you boys can relax and be assured that he is getting whatever help he needs.

    _____

Tears of a Tiger Vocabulary Worksheet Assignment 4 Continued

9. Well, I probably shouldn't tell you boys this, but he *is* getting some outside counseling. I tell you this in the strictest of confidences, because you seem to be so <u>genuinely</u> concerned. So you boys can relax and be assured that he is getting whatever help he needs.

_____

10. Well, I probably shouldn't tell you boys this, but he *is* getting some outside counseling. I tell you this in the strictest of confidences, because you seem to be so genuinely concerned. So you boys can relax and be <u>assured</u> that he is getting whatever help he needs.

_____

Part II: Determining the Meaning -- Match the vocabulary words to their dictionary definitions.

____ 1. VERBALIZE   A. Actually; really; authentically

____ 2. GRIEVING   B. Unable to be avoided or escaped; certain

____ 3. SUICIDE   C. Guaranteed; sure; certain

____ 4. ELIMINATE   D. The process of growing worse, weakening, or declining

____ 5. PATIENT   E. Feelings of assurance that a secret will be kept

____ 6. INEVITABLE   F. Experiencing or expressing sorrow

____ 7. DETERIORATION   G. Having calm endurance

____ 8. CONFIDENCES   H. To express in words

____ 9. GENUINELY   I. To get rid of; remove

____ 10. ASSURED   J. The act of intentionally killing oneself

VOCABULARY ASSIGNMENT 5 *Tears of a Tiger*

Part I: Using Prior Knowledge and Contextual Clues

Below are the sentences in which the vocabulary words appear in the text. Read the sentence. Use any clues you can find in the sentence combined with your prior knowledge, and write what you think the underlined words mean on the lines provided.

1. Well, he's been doing a lot more "acting out" lately. He's always been a cheerful, good-natured kid, with very few <u>inhibitions</u>, which sometimes does not lead to the best classroom behavior.

   _____

2. Andy will stand up on a table and sing "God Bless America" at the top of his lungs if he's giving a report on patriotism. The kids love it, and most of the times the teachers at least <u>tolerate</u> it.

   _____

3. There seem to be more of these kinds of <u>incidents</u> lately, not at all like the Andy we know and care about.

   _____

4. When he's not causing noticeable <u>disturbances</u>, he's somewhat withdrawn.

   _____

5. Let me ask you this--and please don't misunderstand my <u>intentions</u> or think that I'm trying to intrude into the personal life of your family--but wasn't Andy seeing a counselor about possible problems that may have been caused by his involvement in that accident?

   _____

6. Let me ask you this--and please don't misunderstand my intentions or think that I'm trying to <u>intrude</u> into the personal life of your family--but wasn't Andy seeing a counselor about possible problems that may have been caused by his involvement in that accident?

   _____

7. We gonna electrify your senses and <u>bombard</u> your brain with the sounds that make you want to get down!

   _____

8. [Andy] Do you remember that boy in the next cabin? He was about twelve, and we played on the beach together every day. [Mother] <u>Vaguely</u>. Yes, now that you mention it. I remember you playing with an older boy quite a bit.

   _____

9. [Andy] I didn't bring this up to tell you about a dumb stunt I pulled when I was nine. . . . [Mother] Well this is quite a <u>revelation</u>. You're right. I probably *would* have punished you. No doubt about it.

   _____

55

Tears of a Tiger Vocabulary Worksheet Assignment 5 Continued

Part II: Determining the Meaning -- Match the vocabulary words to their dictionary definitions.

____ 1. INHIBITIONS   A. To put or force in inappropriately, especially without permission

____ 2. TOLERATE   B. To endure; to put up with

____ 3. INCIDENTS   C. Not clearly; hazily; somewhat

____ 4. DISTURBANCES   D. Objectives; motives

____ 5. INTENTIONS   E. Outbreaks of disorder; commotion

____ 6. INTRUDE   F. Conscious or unconscious restraint of a behavior

____ 7. BOMBARD   G. To attack or assail, as with artillery or rapid fire

____ 8. VAGUELY   H. An enlightening or astonishing disclosure

____ 9. REVELATION   I. Minor events

VOCABULARY ASSIGNMENT 6 *Tears of a Tiger*

Part I: Using Prior Knowledge and Contextual Clues

Below are the sentences in which the vocabulary words appear in the text. Read the sentence. Use any clues you can find in the sentence combined with your prior knowledge, and write what you think the underlined words mean on the lines provided.

1. [Andy] You didn't even come to one of my games this year! Not one! [Dad] Well, you know how hectic my schedule is. Besides, I've seen you in the yard when you shoot hoops with your friends. I know you're good.

   _____

2. [Dad] But back to the subject at hand--this absolutely reprehensible report card! [Andy] . . . I know my report card stinks. . . .

   _____

3. [Dad] But I expect to see some major improvements in these last couple of months of school. Or I shall have to take some severe punitive measures. [Andy] . . . What else can you do to punish me?

   _____

4. Well, son, let me tell you. My father named me Ezekiel Jeremiah Jackson--two strong Bible names--he had great ambitions for me. But that name turned out to be a detriment rather than an asset to me. . . . it was almost impossible to be taken seriously in the business world with a name like "Ezekiel."

   _____

5. Well, son, let me tell you. My father named me Ezekiel Jeremiah Jackson--two strong Bible names--he had great ambitions for me. But that name turned out to be a detriment rather than an asset to me.

   _____

6. [Andy] Maybe I don't wanna be acceptable to white folks. [Dad] But you *must*! That's the only way to make it in this world--to assimilate into the society in which we live. *That's* why you must pull up your grades and improve your attitude. That is the key to success.

   _____

7. I'm not taking "no" for an answer. You *will* show substantial improvement. I will not accept anything less than maximum effort.

   _____

8. There is no way that your counselor could have seen the future. I'm sure she would have suggested our number had she known the severity of Andy's problems.

   _____

Tears of a Tiger Vocabulary Worksheet Assignment 6 Continued

Part II: Determining the Meaning -- Match the vocabulary words to their dictionary definitions.

____ 1.   HECTIC   A. Become a part of the main or dominant culture

____ 2.   REPREHENSIBLE   B. Punishing

____ 3.   PUNITIVE   C. A cause of loss, damage, disadvantage, or injury

____ 4.   DETRIMENT   D. A useful and desirable thing or quality

____ 5.   ASSET   E. Characterized by intense activity, confusion, or haste

____ 6.   ASSIMILATE   F. Deserving of reproof, rebuke, or censure; blameworthy

____ 7.   SUBSTANTIAL   G. Intensity or sharpness

____ 8.   SEVERITY   H. Of ample or considerable amount

VOCABULARY ANSWER KEY - *Tears of a Tiger*

	1	2	3	4	5	6
1	G	G	B	H	F	E
2	I	F	F	F	B	F
3	H	B	H	J	I	B
4	D	C	C	I	E	C
5	C	A	E	G	D	D
6	F	E	D	B	A	A
7	B	D	A	D	G	H
8	E	H	G	E	C	G
9	A			A	H	

DAILY LESSONS

LESSON ONE

Objectives
1. To introduce the *Tears of a Tiger* unit
2. To distribute books, study questions, and other related materials
3. To preview the vocabulary and study questions for Assignment 1
4. To begin Assignment 1

Activity #1
Find a newspaper or magazine article about a teen or group of teens who died while in high school. Try to find an article that tells about the event and also gets the perspectives of other students, teachers, and family members to show how the event of a teen death affects more than those directly involved. Topics to look for include drugs, alcohol, racing/reckless driving, car accidents, suicide, etc. Often times teen magazines will do a feature about an event like this, so be sure to look in *Seventeen, Teen People, YM*, and other teen-oriented magazines for an article as well as in local and national newspapers. If possible, try to find an article about a teen death near your school to help create a larger impact on your students.

Make copies of the article to hand out to your students. Have students take turns reading out loud while others follow along. Once you have completed the article, ask your students to think about how the death of the teen impacted others in the school and community. Spend some time talking about why the death of a young person can often times be more difficult to deal with than the death of an older adult.

Transition: Once you have discussed the way teen deaths impact the community and how they are often very difficult to deal with, tell your students they will be reading a book called *Tears of a Tiger*. Explain to students this book is written from several different points of view and deals with a deadly car accident and the reaction of the students at Hazelwood High School.

Activity #2
Distribute the Raising Awareness project assignment sheet. Discuss the directions in detail.

Note: Some schools may allow for these projects to be displayed around the school to raise awareness about serious teen issues. If your school allows this, select your best project to display around school. If not, display the projects in your room.

Activity #3
Distribute the materials students will use in this unit. Explain in detail how students are to use these materials.

Study Guides Students should read the study guide questions for each reading assignment prior to beginning the reading assignment to get a feeling for what events and ideas are important in the section they are about to read. After reading the section, students will (as a class or individually) answer the questions to review the important events and ideas from that section of the book. Students should keep the study guides as study materials for the unit test. Review the study questions for Assignment 1 while you're looking at the study guides.

Vocabulary Prior to reading a reading assignment, students will do vocabulary work related to the section of the book they are about to read. Following the completion of the reading of the book, there will be a vocabulary review of all the words used in the vocabulary assignments. Students should keep their vocabulary work as study materials for the unit test. Do Assignment 1 together orally to show students how to do the vocabulary worksheets.

Reading Assignment Sheet You need to fill in the reading assignment sheet to let students know by when their reading has to be completed. You can either write the assignment sheet up on a side blackboard or bulletin board and leave it there for students to see each day, or you can make copies for each student to have. In either case, you should advise students to become very familiar with the reading assignments so they know what is expected of them.

Extra Activities Center The Unit Resource Materials portion of this LitPlan contains suggestions for an extra library of related books and articles in your classroom as well as crossword and word search puzzles. Make an extra activities center in your room where you will keep these materials for students to use. (Bring the books and articles in from the library and keep several copies of the puzzles on hand.) Explain to students that these materials are available for students to use when they finish reading assignments or other class work early.

Non-fiction Assignment Sheet Explain to students that they each are to read at least one non-fiction piece from the in-class library at some time during the unit. Students will fill out a Non-fiction Assignment Sheet after completing the reading to help you (the teacher) evaluate their reading experiences and to help the students think about and evaluate their own reading experiences.

Books Each school has its own rules and regulations regarding student use of school books. Advise students of the procedures that are normal for your school. Preview the book. Look at the covers, frontmatter, and index.

Activity #4
Tell students that they should read Assignment 1 prior to the next class period. Give them the remainder of this class (if time remains) to complete this assignment.

RAISING AWARENESS PROJECT *Tears of a Tiger*

PROMPT
While reading *Tears of a Tiger* you will encounter many serious issues that teens are forced to deal with on a regular basis. The goal of your project is to find a creative way to make other students more aware of one of the serious issues discussed in the novel. Follow all of the instructions on this sheet to receive the highest possible grade. All projects will be presented to the class and displayed for others to see.

PREWRITING
Think about the serious issues that are discussed in the novel (depression, suicide, physical abuse, racial stereotyping, drinking and driving, etc). Select one of these issues to cover in your project. Remember, you will be presenting research-based information in your project, so try to pick a topic that interests you.

Once you have selected a topic, begin conducting research for your project. You will want to include startling facts/statistics, warning signs, what to do if you suspect a problem with a friend, what to do if it's happening to you, hotlines/websites to visit for help, etc. You will also need to find powerful quotes from the novel related to your topic to include in your project. Highlight these as you read to avoid having to look for them later.

DRAFTING
Decide what type of project will best inform your student body about the issue. Ideas include, but are not limited to, posters, a segment/commercial for the school morning show, brochures, or a website you create to be linked to your school site.

Once you have selected the type of project you will be doing, begin putting your research and information from the novel together in an organized manner. You will want to display your information in a way that is both attractive and informative. Remember, you should come up with something that grabs the attention of students and makes them want to learn more about the topic you are covering.

PROMPT
When you finish the rough draft of your project, ask a parent or teacher to look it over. After viewing your rough draft, he/she should tell you what he/she liked best about your work, which parts were difficult to understand, and ways in which your work could be improved. Use this information to make any necessary changes to your project.

PROOFREADING
Do a final proofreading of your project double-checking your grammar, spelling, organization, and the clarity of your ideas.

LESSON TWO

Objectives
1. To review main ideas, events, and vocabulary of Assignment 1
2. To create a visual display that will be used as a during and after reading strategy
3. To help students organize the events of the story and the feelings and experiences of each character

Activity #1
Give students a few minutes to formulate answers for the study guide questions for Assignment 1 and then discuss the answers to the questions in detail. Write the answers on the board or overhead transparency so students can have the correct answers for study purposes.

NOTE: It is a good practice in public speaking and leadership skills for individual students to take charge of leading the discussions of the study questions. Perhaps a different student could go to the front of the class and lead the discussion each day that the study questions are discussed in this unit. Of course, you should guide the discussion when appropriate and try to fill in any gaps students may leave. The study questions could really be handled in a number of different ways, including in small groups with group reports following. Occasionally you may want to use the multiple choice questions as quizzes to check students' reading comprehension. As a short review now and then, students could pair up for the first (or last, if you have time left at the end of a class period) few minutes of class to quiz each other from the study questions. Mix up methods of reviewing the materials and checking comprehension throughout the unit so students don't get bored just answering the questions the same way each day. Variety in methods will also help address the different learning styles of your students.

Alternative Activity: Depending on the time you have in class and the level of your students, you may want to use the time after reviewing the study guide questions to place your students in Literature Circles to complete the Extra Discussion Questions for the reading section you just finished. Simply put students into small groups and have them answer the questions together, coming together afterwards to hold a class discussion about the questions you covered. This way students can work through the questions as they appear in the reading and can work through the whole book questions at the completion of the novel.

Activity #2
Review the vocabulary answers from the reading. Make sure students write down the correct answers.

Activity #3
Tears of a Tiger is told from the perspective of several speakers. With so many different speakers and the story and feelings of each person jumping from page to page, the events in the story can get confusing for students. Students are also easily confused with the thoughts and feelings of each character, and where they stand in dealing with Rob and Andy's deaths.

To help students with organizing the actions and feelings of each character, have students work in groups to create a cut-out of each character. Place students in groups of two or three and assign each group a character from the story. Give them a large piece of bulletin board paper and have them make a cut-out of that character. Students may want to trace someone to make their cut-out life-size, or sketch it by hand. Have students use markers to draw clothes and facial features for their character cut-out. After the character cut-outs are complete, hang them on the walls of your classroom. Place a piece of large construction paper over the character's head with his or her name at the top. Leave plenty of blank space on the paper so that students can add personality traits, thoughts, feelings, emotions, and actions of the characters as they read the novel.

Activity #4
Take a few moments to add information to the character cut-outs from Assignment 1. Include information like character actions, memories, thoughts, feelings, interactions with other characters, opinions, etc. The point is to provide enough information from each reading assignment on the construction paper over the character so that students can stay organized with what is going on with each speaker in the text.

LESSON THREE

<u>Objectives</u>
1. To have students research and read non-fiction related to the book to help connect the book to real life
2. To broaden students' knowledge about topics related to the book
3. To preview the vocabulary and study questions for Assignment 2
4. To read Assignment 2

<u>Activity #1</u>
Take students to the library or media center. With students, brainstorm a list of non-fiction topics that could be related to *Tears of a Tiger*. A short list to get you started is included below.

* Depression
* Alcohol use with teens
* Suicide
* Racial inequality
* Peer pressure
* Real stories of teens who have had to deal with the death of a friend
* Real stories of teens who have survived a suicide attempt
* Real stories of teens who have survived an accident related to alcohol
* How teenagers can get help
* Communication between teenagers and parents
* Physical abuse at home
* Organizations that offer help for teenagers who are depressed or suicidal
* Criminal punishments for underage alcohol consumption and accidents
* Mentality of teens and the idea that nothing will happen to them
* Dealing with the death of a friend or schoolmate

<u>Activity #2</u>
Distribute the Non-fiction Assignment Sheet to students. Explain that students should choose a non-fiction topic related to *Tears of a Tiger*. They should read a substantial article related to that topic and complete the Non-fiction Assignment Sheet for that article. Students may use magazines, newspapers, and the Internet as sources.

<u>Activity #3</u>
Bring the class back together and have each student tell what he/she read about.

Note: Compiling the Non-fiction Assignment Sheets into a booklet makes a nice follow-up activity and a handy reference for students.

<u>Activity #4</u>
Review the study questions and vocabulary for Assignment 2 orally together in class. Tell students that they should read Assignment 2 prior to the next class period. Give them the remainder of this class (if time remains) to complete this assignment.

NON-FICTION ASSIGNMENT SHEET
(To be completed after reading the required non-fiction article)

Name_____ Date _____

Title of Non-fiction Read _____

Written By _____ Publication Date _____

I. Factual Summary: Write a short summary of the piece you read.

II. Vocabulary
1. With which vocabulary words in the piece did you encounter some degree of difficulty?

2. How did you resolve your lack of understanding with these words?

III. Interpretation: What was the main point the author wanted you to get from reading this work?

IV. Criticism
    1. With which points of the piece did you agree or find easy to accept? Why?

    2. With which points of the piece did you disagree or find difficult to believe? Why?

V. Personal Response: What do you think about this piece? OR How does this piece influence your ideas/thinking?

LESSON FOUR

Objectives
1. To review main ideas, events, and vocabulary of Assignment 2
2. To help students organize the events of the story and the feelings and experiences of each character
3. To help students make inferences from the text
4. To bridge a connection between events in the novel to students' lives

Activity #1
Have students answer the study guide questions for reading Assignment 2 as previously directed.

Activity #2
Review the vocabulary answers from the reading. Make sure students write down the correct answers.

Activity #3
Add events from the reading to character cut-outs as previously described.

Activity #4
Talk to your students about making inferences in a text. Explain that though the author doesn't always come right out and give the reader information, she is usually giving clues for the reader to make inferences about the characters and their lives. Tell your students that they will be making inferences about Andy's relationship with his family based on reading assignments one and two.

Distribute the attached Venn Diagram to students. If your class is unfamiliar with this type of graphic organizer, you may want to spend a few minutes showing them how to fill it out. Explain to your students that they will be comparing and contrasting Andy's relationships with his family to their own relationships with their own families. Instruct your students to make inferences from the text to determine what Andy's home life is like. Encourage them to use both reading assignments to find direct quotations from the novel to place in their Venn Diagram. Suggestions include the reaction Andy's parents have toward the accident, how they help their son deal with his guilt, their involvement in his school life, their involvement in his extra-curricular activities, etc. As they are making inferences regarding Andy's relationship with his parents, they should also be using the Venn Diagram to compare and contrast his home life with their own. After students have completed their Venn Diagrams, ask them to write a short reflection about their findings at the bottom of the page in the space provided. When your class has finished, you may want to take a few moments to allow students to share their findings, placing an emphasis on talking about Andy's relationship with his family and how that affects him during this difficult time in his life.

Tears of a Tiger Venn Diagram: Family Relationships

You

Andy

Overall Findings: _____

LESSON FIVE

Objectives
1. To help connect ideas in the book to real life
2. To examine the effect Rob's death had on the characters in the story
3. To help students understand cause and effect relationships in the novel
4. To preview the vocabulary and study questions for Assignment 3
5. To read Assignment 3

Activity #1
The students at Hazelwood High School are shocked to learn of Rob's death and have a difficult time understanding how this accident could have happened to someone so young. Take the first part of class to talk to your students about teen psychology. Use a psychology textbook or articles from the internet to aid in a class discussion about how teens process information and apply it to their own lives. You should try to connect problems students are faced with in the novel to psychological explanations of teens in real life. A short list of ideas is included to help get you started.

   * Understanding that teenagers can and do die: Rhonda writing in her English essay that she didn't know people her age could die

   * The "it can't happen to me" idea: Even though Andy and his friends knew better than to drink and drive, they never really thought anything bad would happen to them

   * The effects of peer pressure: B.J. knew better than to let his friends drink and drive, but didn't want to be thought of as "uncool" if he spoke up about it

   * Teens not learning from the mistakes of others: Even though Andy and his friends knew drinking and driving could be deadly, they couldn't learn from the accidents of others

Activity #2
Talk to your students about cause and effect. Explain that one event usually causes several different effects. Ask your students to think about how Rob's death changed the lives of students at Hazelwood High School and the surrounding community. Distribute the Cause and Effect Chart to your students. Ask them to write "Rob's Death" in one of the center squares labeled "Cause." Have them then write the effect his death had on the characters in the novel in the "Effect" boxes branching off the main "Cause" box.

Encourage your students to use details from the text when completing this chart. Some of the characters may not have had a direct reaction to his death, but are still effected in some way (eg. Andy's parents having to help their son cope). You will also want to explain to your class that they are only completing half of the chart at this time. They will complete the rest of the chart at the end of the novel, so it should be kept in a safe place until then.

(continued on next page)

Activity #3
Once your students have had sufficient time to complete the chart, bring the class back together and hold a class discussion about the effect of Rob's death on the community. Try to get your students to think about how each character in the novel has been changed in some way. You may also want to point out that the author's style helps readers in understanding how each character is dealing with events in the novel due to the various perspectives used in her writing.

Activity #4
Review the study questions and vocabulary for Assignment 3 orally together in class. Tell students that they should read Assignment 3 prior to the next class period. Give them the remainder of this class (if time remains) to complete this assignment.

Cause and Effect Chart: *Tears of a Tiger*

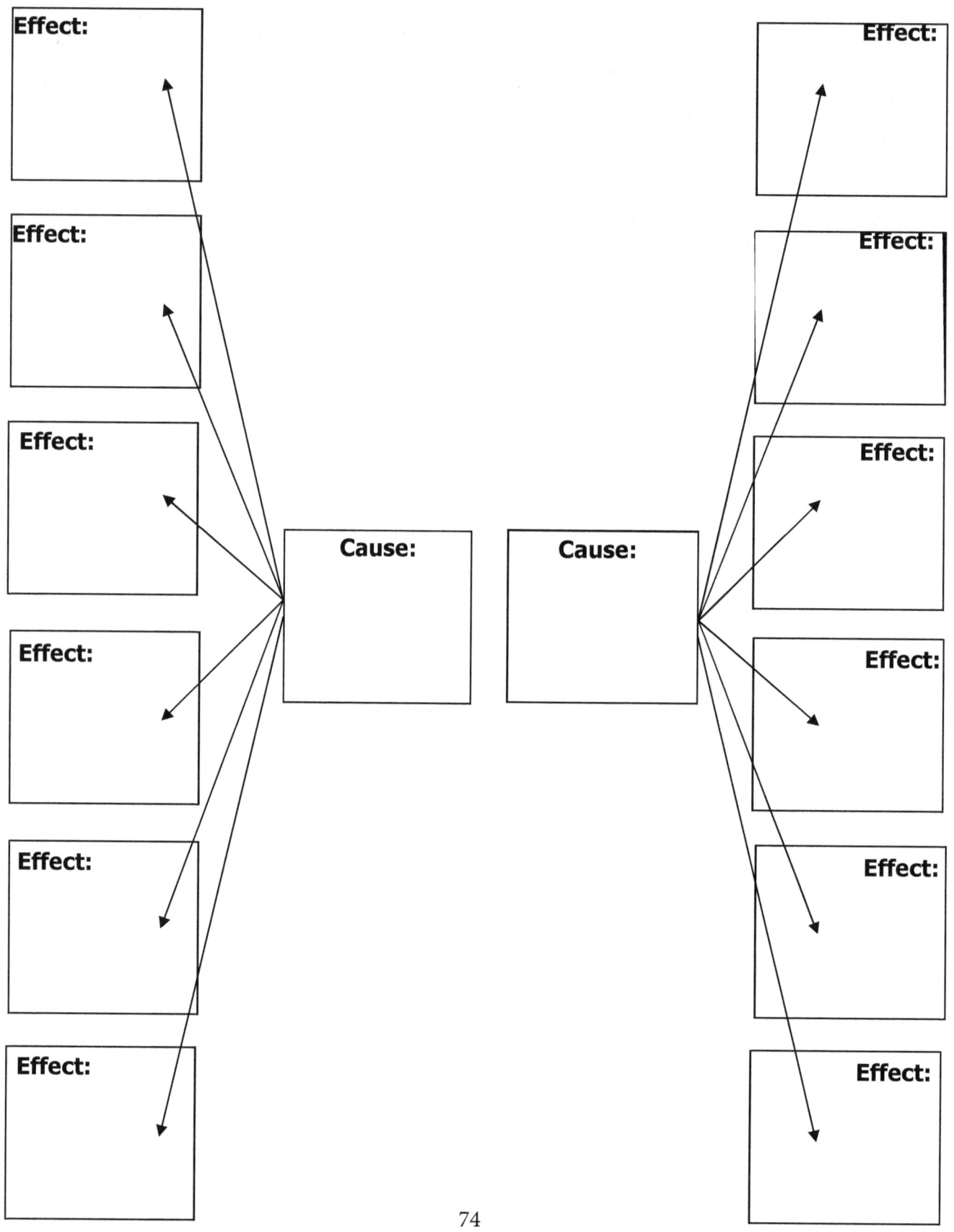

LESSON SIX

Objectives
1. To review main ideas, events, and vocabulary of Assignment 3
2. To help students organize the events of the story and the feelings and experiences of each character
3. To preview study questions and vocabulary for Assignment 4
4. To read Assignment 4
5. To evaluate students' oral reading

Activity #1
Have students answer the study guide questions for Assignment 3 as previously directed. Preview the questions for Assignment 4 while you have the study guides out.

Activity #2
Review the vocabulary answers from the reading. Make sure students write down the correct answers.

Activity #3
Add events from the reading to character cut-outs as previously described.

Activity #4
Do the vocabulary worksheet for Assignment 4 together in class.

Activity #5
Have students read Assignment 4 of *Tears of a Tiger* out loud in class. You probably know the best way to get readers with your class; pick students at random, ask for volunteers, or use whatever method works best for your group. If you have not yet completed an oral reading evaluation for your students, this would be a good opportunity to do so. A form is included with this unit for your convenience.

ORAL READING EVALUATION *Tears of a Tiger*

Name_____ Class _____ Date _____

SKILL	EXCELLENT	GOOD	AVERAGE	FAIR	POOR
Fluency	5	4	3	2	1
Clarity	5	4	3	2	1
Audibility	5	4	3	2	1
Pronunciation	5	4	3	2	1
_____	5	4	3	2	1
_____	5	4	3	2	1

Total _____ Grade _____

Comments:

LESSON SEVEN

Objectives
To bring ideas from the book into real life

Activity #1
This day has been set aside for a guest speaker. Invite one or more of the following people from your community to speak to your class:

* A representative from a suicide prevention organization
* A psychologist who frequently works with teens
* A survivor from a drunk driving accident
* A police officer who has handled incidents resulting from teen alcohol or drug abuse
* A motivational speaker to encourage students to find outlets for their problems
* A teen who has dealt with the sudden death of a friend
* A teen who has attempted suicide
* A representative from any teen outreach program

Divide your class time according to how many speakers you're able to acquire. Remember to allow time for students to ask questions. Let each speaker know how much time he/she will have for the presentation. Allow for time at the end of the class for students to make connections with what they have learned from the speakers with what they have read in *Tears of a Tiger*.

Follow Up: Be sure you and your students write thank you notes to each of your guests. At the very least, get a thank you card for each guest and have each of your students sign it (with any personal responses, if there is room).

LESSON EIGHT

Objectives
> 1. To make students stop and think about their decision-making processes and whether or not those processes are appropriate
> 2. To express personal opinions using a topic discussed in *Tears of a Tiger*
> 3. To improve students' writing ability

Activity

In *Tears of a Tiger* the lives of many students are changed due to a bad decision made by Andy and his friends to drink and drive. Even though one of the teens later admits he knew better than to drink and drive, he still made the choice to ignore the consequences and follow through with his decision. In this assignment, students will express their opinions as to why teens often make poor decisions, even when they know the consequences could be dangerous. Students will also be mimicking the style of writing seen in the novel by applying various media and speakers to complete their assignment. Distribute Writing Assignment 1 and use the attached rubric to give feedback to your students.

WRITING ASSIGNMENT #1 *Tears of a Tiger*

PROMPT
Andy and his friends are aware that drinking and driving is dangerous, but they still make the decision to get behind the wheel after drinking illegally. As a reader, you are able to see how this bad decision affects so many others in the school and surrounding community through the multiple perspectives the writer gives. Your assignment is to mimic the author's writing style by using a variety of speakers and media to address the issue of why teens sometimes overlook the consequences and follow through with a bad decision.

PREWRITING
Think about the poor decisions teens sometimes make despite knowing the negative consequences. Make a short list of a few examples of harmful decisions teens make, even though they often know better (drinking and driving, drug use, racing, etc). Next, determine which media you will use in your writing. You may want to use examples found in the book like overheard conversations, diary entries, and school assignments or use more contemporary media like blogs, instant messages, text messages, or comments on online profiles. You will also need to create a few characters of your own to talk back and forth about your assigned topic.

DRAFTING
This writing assignment will not look like a traditional essay. You will need to use at least three different media to address the assigned topic, with a minimum of five speakers. Be sure to clearly label what format you are using and designate where each section begins and ends.

As you are writing, remember to use first person point of view, but from the eyes of the characters you created. You will want to use details and to make your writing as authentic as possible. You should also provide your readers with insights into the topic so they are able to understand why you feel teens make poor decisions at times. Remember to use your different speakers to make strong points to support your personal opinion.

PROMPT
When you finish the rough draft of your composition, ask a student who sits near you to read it. After reading your rough draft, he/she should tell you what he/she liked best about your work, which parts were difficult to understand, and ways in which your work could be improved. Re-read your paper considering your critic's comments, and make the corrections you think are necessary. Ask your classmate what he/she thought of each of the characters/events you chose for your assignment.

PROOFREADING
Do a final proofreading of your paper double-checking your grammar, spelling, organization, and the clarity of your ideas.

WRITING EVALUATION FORM - *Tears of a Tiger*

Name _____ Date _____ Writing Assignment # _____

Grade _____

Circle One For Each Item:

Variety of Media:	excellent	good	fair	poor
Multiple Speakers:	excellent	good	fair	poor
Insight Into Topic:	excellent	good	fair	poor
Grammar:	excellent	good	fair	poor
Spelling:	excellent	good	fair	poor
Punctuation:	excellent	good	fair	poor
Legibility:	excellent	good	fair	poor
_____:	excellent	good	fair	poor
_____:	excellent	good	fair	poor

Strengths:

Weaknesses:

Comments/Suggestions:

LESSON NINE

<u>Objectives</u>
1. To review main ideas, events, and vocabulary of Assignment 4
2. To help students organize the events of the story and the feelings and experiences of each character
3. To closely examine one of the themes of the novel

<u>Activity #1</u>
Have students answer the study guide questions for Assignment 4 as previously directed.

<u>Activity #2</u>
Review the vocabulary answers from the reading. Make sure students write down the correct answers.

<u>Activity #3</u>
Add events from the reading to character cut-outs as previously described.

<u>Activity #4</u>
Several speakers in the novel mention discrimination they experience and witness on a regular basis. One of the underlying themes of the novel is the unfair treatment and altered expectations black people tend to receive. Take a moment to talk to your students about how several characters express their frustrations about the unfair ways they are treated due to their race.

After a short discussion to get students thinking about the subject, place students into small groups. Give each group several index cards and instruct them to find specific examples from the text where a character mentions being the victim of stereotype, dealing with lowered expectations, or being treated unfairly due to race. Have your students write the excerpt from the novel dealing with the incident on one side of the card, and place the reaction or affect it has on that person on the other side. Make sure students look for examples in all of the reading assignments covered to date.

After students have had enough time to find several examples from the text, bring the class back together to share the findings. In addition to sharing the examples students found, you may also want to direct students to think about why the author included this topic in her novel. You should also ask your students to determine if the type of discriminatory treatment seen in the novel still takes place today.

Note: *As a follow up to the activity, you may want to hang the index cards in your room to display. You can create a class mobile on discrimination and add to it as students encounter other examples of discrimination in the novel.*

LESSON TEN

Objectives
1. To help understand the effect of the author's writing style on the reader
2. To encourage students to make personal connections with topics covered in the text
3. To preview the vocabulary and study questions for Assignment 5
4. To read Assignment 5

Activity #1
Ask students to reread the poems the characters from the story wrote for their English assignment. Tell students they will need to write a poem of their own about a problem they face as a teen. They can write about something simple like dealing with the daily drama of school life, to something more complex like dealing with difficult home situations or personal decisions.

Activity #2
After students have had time to write their poems, ask students to share what they wrote. Remind students that when listening to the poems of others they should be respectful to their peers and understand that sharing a poem can often be a difficult process.

Activity #3
After students have shared their poems, ask your class to reflect on the assignment as a whole. Encourage them to think about how hearing the poems of their peers provided them with additional insight into the lives of others. You may also want to point out that hearing multiple perspectives can often be more powerful than hearing something from only one point of view.

Transition this discussion to the novel by asking students to think about the author's style of writing and how it adds to the book. Encourage your students to talk about how the novel is enhanced due to the different style of writing the author uses and how they are able to better understand the topics she discusses through experiencing the thoughts and feelings of multiple characters.

Activity #4
Review the study questions and vocabulary for Assignment 5 orally together in class. Tell students that they should read Assignment 5 prior to the next class period. Give them the remainder of this class (if time remains) to complete this assignment.

LESSON ELEVEN

Objectives
1. To review main ideas, events, and vocabulary of Assignment 5
2. To help students organize the events of the story and the feelings and experiences of each character
3. To help students analyze Andy's intricate character
4. To preview the vocabulary and study questions for Assignment 6
5. To read Assignment 6

Activity #1
Have students answer the study guide questions for Assignment 5 as previously directed.

Activity #2
Review the vocabulary answers from the reading. Make sure students write down the correct answers.

Activity #3
Add events from the reading to character cut-outs as previously described.

Activity #4
Give students construction paper, scissors, and markers. Ask students to cut a head shape out of the piece of construction paper. Talk to your students about the two sides to Andy- the side he shows his friends and the side he keeps hidden deep within. Instruct students to write descriptions of the Andy his family, friends, and teachers see on one side of the head and descriptions of the Andy that stays hidden inside on the other. Encourage students to use quotes from the novel to help support their descriptions.

Activity #5
After students have finished working on their assignment, hold a class discussion about the different sides of Andy. Have students use their descriptions from their head cut-outs to help guide them in a class discussion. You may also want to prompt students to make predictions about what will happen to Andy if he is unable to show more of the person he is inside and less of the person he pretends to be on the outside. Allow students to comment on whether or not any of the characters in the novel see through his exterior behavior to the struggle he is dealing with inside. Have them cite evidence from the story to support their answers.

Note: You may want to hang the students' Andy heads from the ceiling of your room so students are able to see other examples of the two sides of Andy.

Activity #6
Review the study questions and vocabulary for Assignment 6 orally together in class. Tell students that they should read Assignment 6 prior to the next class period. Give them the remainder of this class (if time remains) to complete this assignment.

LESSON TWELVE

Objectives
> 1. To review main ideas, events, and vocabulary of Assignment 6
> 2. To help students organize the events of the story and the feelings and experiences of each character
> 3. To help students understand cause and effect relationships in the novel
> 4. To help students analyze the main events in the novel

Activity #1
Have students answer the study guide questions for Assignment 6 as previously directed.

Activity #2
Review the vocabulary answers from the reading. Make sure students write down the correct answers.

Activity #3
Add events from the reading to character cut-outs as previously described. Take this time to go over the information on these cut-outs as a review of the events each character experienced throughout the novel.

Activity #4
Have students take out their cause and effect charts from lesson five. In the second "Cause" box, ask students to write "Andy's Suicide." Next, have them fill out the effect his death had on others in the novel in the boxes branching off the main box in the center. After students have finished, hold a class discussion about how two events in the novel changed the lives of so many others. You may also want to ask students to think about the message the author was trying to convey in her novel.

LESSON THIRTEEN

Objectives
To analyze the events in the novel that led to the climax of the story

Activity #1
Place students in small groups and distribute construction paper and markers. Ask students to think of the events in the novel that led to Andy's decision to commit suicide. Tell students they should work together to create a timeline of events from the novel that led up to Andy's suicide. Instruct them to place examples of characters trying to help Andy and examples of Andy trying to reach out for help on the timeline as well.

After groups have completed their timelines, bring the class back together to share their information. Hold a class discussion on whether or not anyone could have prevented Andy from committing suicide and if he showed any signs characters might have missed. Talk about why Andy made the choice he did and why he thought it was the only solution. You may also want to discuss why some characters were unable to see the signs Andy showed of his deep depression.

LESSON FOURTEEN

Objectives
1. To bring ideas from the book into real life
2. To allow students to discover effective ways to communicate with others

Activity #1
Throughout the book Andy struggles with his depression. Though he is suffering, he keeps his feelings bottled up inside and puts on a show for everyone to make them think he is all right. Before he commits suicide he tries to reach out to others in his life to explain how he feels, but no one understands exactly what he is going through. Instead, his struggle builds to a point where he can no longer take it, thus resulting in his suicide.

Begin this activity by holding a class discussion on communication between teenagers and parents. Ask students to talk about their own relationships with their parents, pointing out what specifically is difficult for teenagers and parents in effective communication. You may also want to ask students about communication with other adults in contrast with communication with their peers. Ask them to think about whether talking to other adults is sometimes easier than a parent, or if peer conversation can ever be difficult as well. Transition the discussion to talk about Andy's problem in talking with others in his life. Brainstorm a list of examples in the novel when Andy wants to show others he is struggling, but can't effectively communicate his feelings.

Activity #2
After the discussion, break students into small groups. Tell students they will be conducting a daytime talk show with Andy, his parents, and other characters in the novel as the guests. Have each group select a famous talk show (Oprah, Dr. Phil, Maury, Montel, Greg Behrendt, etc.) and determine who in the group will play the host, Andy, and the other guests. Once students have determined roles, have them begin to write a script. Encourage students to think about the format of most daytime talk shows and use that as their guide. Tell students to remain as close to the text and true personality of the characters they are playing as possible. Remind students that the point of the assignment is to create and model effective communication between Andy and others in the novel. You may also want to remind students to keep the material school appropriate.

After students have had time to write a short script, allow each group to host their talk show in front of the class. Afterwards, have students rate how well each group did in portraying effective communication between Andy and other characters.

LESSON FIFTEEN

Objectives
    1. To practice writing to inform
    2. To improve students' writing ability
    3. To analyze communications skills and the effects of poor communication

Activity #1
Students have spent a sufficient amount of class time reflecting on Andy's suicide and the effect it had on others. They have also analyzed the reason Andy made the decision he did and looked at how the result may have been different had he been able to communicate his feelings to others in his life. At this time, students should be ready to write an essay to inform someone about the importance of good communication. Distribute Writing Assignment 2 to your students and use the following rubric to provide feedback.

WRITING ASSIGNMENT #2 *Tears of a Tiger*

PROMPT
Andy puts on a brave front, trying to convince everyone in his life that he's doing okay. As the reader, you see as Andy slowly slips deeper into depression as a result of not being able to communicate with anyone in his life. In his final moments of desperation, Andy tries to find someone to talk to who will understand his pain, but he has no luck, resulting in his decision to commit suicide. Your assignment it to write to inform others on the importance of good communication.

PREWRITING
Using your notes/information from the speaker, non-fiction assignment, and other class assignments, brainstorm reasons why good communication is important. Try to include facts and statistics for support, while using several examples from the novel as well. You will also want to think of all the people Andy could have gone to for support. He had his friends, family, teachers, coach, and psychologist to help him; he just lacked the ability to communicate and share his struggles until it was too late. You should also remember that Andy wasn't the only person who had trouble communicating. His parents, as well as other characters, missed the chance to talk to Andy when he reached out to them due to their lack of good communication skills or other factors.

DRAFTING
Write an introductory paragraph where you give a thesis statement about why good communication is important. You may want to include in this paragraph a highlight of the support and reasons you will cover in the remainder of your essay.

In the body paragraphs, continue to put forth your reasons why communication is important. Remember to use your facts, statistics, and examples from the text to support your view. Make each new reason a separate paragraph.

In your conclusion paragraph, wrap up your ideas for the reader. Try to end with a strong final statement to leave a lasting impression on your reader.

PROMPT
When you finish the rough draft of your composition, ask a student who sits near you to read it. After reading your rough draft, he/she should tell you what he/she liked best about your work, which parts were difficult to understand, and ways in which your work could be improved. Reread your paper considering your critic's comments, and make the corrections you think are necessary. Ask your classmate what he/she thought of each of the characters/events you chose for your assignment.

PROOFREADING
Do a final proofreading of your paper double-checking your grammar, spelling, organization, and the clarity of your ideas.

WRITING EVALUATION FORM - *Tears of a Tiger*

Name _____ Date _____ Writing Assignment # _____

Grade _____

Circle One For Each Item:

Introduction:	excellent	good	fair	poor
Body Paragraphs:	excellent	good	fair	poor
Conclusion:	excellent	good	fair	poor
Grammar:	excellent	good	fair	poor
Spelling:	excellent	good	fair	poor
Punctuation:	excellent	good	fair	poor
Legibility:	excellent	good	fair	poor
_____:	excellent	good	fair	poor
_____:	excellent	good	fair	poor

Strengths:

Weaknesses:

Comments/Suggestions:

LESSON SIXTEEN

Objectives
    1. To discuss the novel on a deeper than direct-recall level
    2. To prepare students for questions and topics covered on the test
    3. To help students to make personal connections with the text

Activity #1
Choose the questions from the Extra Discussion Questions/Writing Assignments which seem most appropriate for your students. A class discussion of these questions is most effective if students have been given the opportunity to formulate answers to the questions prior to the discussion. To this end, you may either have all the students formulate answers to all the questions, divide your class into groups and assign one or more questions to each group, or you could assign one question to each student in your class. The option you choose will make a difference in the amount of class time needed for this activity.

Note: The use of graphic organizers may be helpful to students in preparing their answers. Encourage them to use any diagrams or graphics that they feel are necessary.

EXTRA DISCUSSION QUESTIONS *Tears of a Tiger*

Interpretive
1. How does the lack of traditional dialogue affect the quality of the book? (ALL)
2. What is the setting, and what does it add to the story? (ALL)
3. What are the main conflicts in the story? Describe each fully. (ALL)
4. Under what genre does the story fall? (ALL)
5. How does the point of view enhance the novel? Give specific examples to support your answer. (ALL)
6. Describe the author's writing style. (ALL)

Critical
7. Andy, Tyrone, and B.J. were very close before the accident. How does their friendship change over the course of the novel? How could the outcome of the novel have been different if the boys had remained close? (ALL)
8. How was each character changed by the events in the novel? (ALL)
9. What is the significance of the title? (ALL)
10. What signs of suicide does Andy show? Could anyone in the novel have known what he was planning to do? Is there anything that could have been done to stop him? (ALL)
11. Monty goes to Andy's grave to say good-bye to his brother. What does he say to him? How was he affected by his brother's decision to kill himself? What has happened to Andy's family since then? (RA6)
12. Analyze the letters Andy's friends write. How is each friend affected by Andy's suicide? (RA6)
13. B.J. is angry because Andy didn't ask for help before killing himself. Is this true? Explain your answer. (RA6)
14. Andy talks about tigers in cages just before he commits suicide. What does he say about these tigers? How are they a metaphor for the way he is feeling? (RA6)
15. Andy describes how he feels about school in Nighttime Cries of Desperation. How does he view all the other students? How is he different from everyone else? (RA6)
16. What does Andy's mother call the accident? How does she deal with the car accident? How does her reaction to the accident affect Andy? (RA5)
17. Compare and contrast Andy and Keisha's relationship with Tyrone and Rhonda's. (RA5)
18. Keisha mentions that Andy has everyone fooled. They all think he's adjusting just fine after the accident, but Keisha sees him as severely depressed. How is Andy able to hide his true feelings from everyone? Why doesn't anyone see that Andy is depressed? (RA5)
19. Andy's teacher calls home to talk to his father about his disruptive behavior. She also mentions he's stopped grooming himself and is very withdrawn. How does Andy's father handle the news? Why does he react in this way? (RA5)
20. Using the main points Keisha makes in her homework essay about the importance of friendship, discuss Keisha's friendship with Andy. (RA4)

21. Keisha says in her English essay, "Sometimes I feel so alone I just want to cry. That's why I'm thankful that I have a good friend like Rhonda, who always has a strong shoulder for me to cry on." Why doesn't Keisha rely on Andy for support? (RA4)

22. Compare and contrast how B.J. and Tyrone deal with the accident with how Andy deals with the accident. (RA4)

23. How does Andy react when other people bring up Rob in conversation? (RA4)

24. Andy's English class studies the play *Macbeth*. During a class discussion on Lady Macbeth's suicide and her husband's change in character over the course of the play, Andy leaves class visibly upset. Why does he get so upset? Use details from the text to support your answer. (RA4)

25. Why does Andy wish he were part of Rob's family? Does this closeness with Rob's family over the years help or hurt Andy in dealing with Rob's death? (RA4)

26. What does Andy's dream about Rob reveal? (RA4)

27. How is Andy's psychologist different in regards to talking about death than others in Andy's life? (RA4)

28. Compare and contrast the way Andy and Keisha each view their relationship. (RA3)

29. Andy describes several instances when he is the victim of stereotyping due to his skin color. How does he deal with these feelings? How does this affect him? (RA3)

30. Why does the author choose to include the English poems each of the characters in the novel wrote? (RA3)

31. Analyze the poem Andy writes for his English class. What does this reveal about what he's feeling? Knowing the poem is worth a large portion of his grade, why doesn't he turn it in? (RA3)

32. Why doesn't Andy try to do well in school? (RA2)

33. Compare and contrast Andy's view of grades with that of his parents. (RA2)

34. What role does basketball play in Andy's healing? (RA2)

35. How does Andy feel after the first home game after Rob's death? How would most people expect him to feel? What does he struggle with after the game? (RA2)

36. Analyze Gerald's English essay about changing the world in Assignment 2. Why does he write about getting rid of peanut butter, Band-Aids, and five dollar bills? What does this say about what he endures in his personal life? (RA2)

37. What can readers infer about Andy's relationship with his parents? Use details from the text to support your answer. (RA2)

38. Andy is able to talk to his coach right after the accident. How does his coach help him deal with his confusion after the accident? What good advice goes his coach give him? What is his coach trying to help him realize? (RA1)

39. How does Andy deal with returning back to school after the accident? What does he confess to his coach about his feelings regarding Rob's death and his role in the car crash? Why does Andy wish he had died in the accident? (RA1)

40. Reread the first edition of The Hazelwood Herald after Rob's death. In what ways did his death affect the rest of the school? How did this one accident make its way into almost every aspect of student life? (RA1)

41. Rhonda writes in her English essay that her most frightening moment was when she learned Rob was dead. Even though she wasn't in the car and wasn't very close to Rob, why was this her most frightening moment? What realizations does Rhonda have after learning of Rob's death? (RA1)

42. What are the main themes of the novel? (ALL)

43. Analyze the way in which the author conveys the events of the novel through a variety of formats. Be sure to discuss the role the more personal formats like phone calls, diary entries, and conversations have with the more factual entries like police statements and newspaper articles. (ALL)

<u>Critical/Personal Response</u>

44. Andy's friends and family are deeply affected by his suicide. Do you think Andy ever stopped to think about how his death would alter the lives of so many people? Explain your answer. (RA6)

45. Andy's friends are shocked that he killed himself. Did you predict that Andy would kill himself at the end of the novel? What clues did the author provide to let you know that Andy was going to do something drastic? (RA6)

46. Andy's father explains the racial struggle he's always had in the business world with such an odd name. What has his father had to do to "fit in" in a predominately white business world? Do you think names play a part in stereotypes now? Explain your answer. (RA6)

47. Andy says, "I don't need college. I don't need basketball. I don't need Keisha. I don't need nothin'!" Can Andy really make it on his own? Why do you think he keeps trying to convince himself he doesn't need anyone? (RA5)

48. Andy's psychologist thinks he has made significant progress and will no longer need regular visits. Do you think Andy is ready to stop seeing his psychologist? Explain why or why not. (RA4)

49. Andy's psychologist suggests he write a letter to Rob's parents, write a letter to Rob, or even consider talking to other teens about drinking and driving as an alternative to suicide. Do you think these methods could help Andy? Explain why or why not. (RA4)

50. Andy admits to his psychologist that he sometimes considers suicide. Why do you think this is? (RA4)

51. Andy's guidance counselor tells him with his grades he probably wouldn't be accepted into law school like he planned. She suggests he pick an easier major and focus on his athletic ability. This bothers Andy and as a result he doesn't really care about his grades. Do you think the guidance counselor was correct in saying what she did to Andy? Was she being realistic or simply prejudiced? Explain your answer. (RA2)

52. Andy says the black kids at school hate the smart kids. He explains if he were making Honor Roll, his friends would laugh at him, so instead he just skates by. Why is this? Should Andy hold back in school to retain his popularity? Explain your answer. (RA2)

53. Andy's parents get on to him for his falling grades. Do you think this is justified? How do your parents handle your grades? (RA2)

54. Andy's psychologist says, "Maybe you're blaming yourself for something that Rob forgives you for." Why do you think it is difficult for Andy to see this point of view? What advice would you offer Andy in dealing with his friend's death? (RA2)

55. How does Andy feel about seeing a psychologist? Do you think he needs to see one? Why or why not? How would you feel if you were in Andy's position? (RA2)

56. Andy's basketball coach says, "You gotta stop punishing yourself." In what ways is Andy punishing himself for his role in the accident? Do you think Andy should continue to punish himself over what happened or try to understand it was beyond his control like his coach suggests? Explain your answer. (RA1)

57. B.J. feels guilty and has trouble understanding why Rob had to die. What reasons does he have to feel guilty? Do you think he is justified in feeling guilty? Explain why or why not. (RA1)

Personal Response

58. Andy struggles to communicate his feelings regarding the accident. The people who notice something is wrong don't take action, and the people he reaches out to don't know how to help. Knowing that deep down Andy really wanted help, how would you handle this problem if one of your friends were depressed? How would you handle this problem if you were a parent and your child were depressed? (ALL)

59. The characters in the novel will forever be haunted by Rob and Andy's deaths. Think about how the choices you make while in high school can affect the rest of your life. How do you deal with the bad decisions you make in your lifetime? Are the choices that you make now something that will haunt you later in life? Give examples to support your answer. (ALL)

60. Andy desperately needed someone to understand his pain and help him get over the accident. If Andy were your friend, what would you say to him to help? (RA6)

61. Andy and his father argue over his grades. His father asks him how he expects to go to college with such poor grades, and Andy points out that college has always been his father's dream, not his. What expectations do your parents have for your future? How do you handle trying to meet their expectations while still trying to live your life in your own way? (RA6)

62. Andy's mother has a difficult time understanding her son and helping him through his struggles. What advice would you offer his mom? What advice would you offer your own parents about helping you in difficult times? (RA5)

63. Keisha writes an essay about the importance of friendship. How important is friendship to you? How much do you rely on your friends for support? (RA4)

64. Andy's teacher says poetry "can say what we're able to feel but unable to put into words ourselves." Do you agree or disagree with this statement? Explain your answer. (RA3)

65. Keisha struggles to understand Andy and support him throughout his depression. If you were Keisha, how would you help your friend deal with something so huge? (RA3)

66. The kids at school resent the smarter students, holding some popular people back from showing their intelligence in order to be cool. How do others view the intelligent students at your school? Is it cooler to just get by than it is to succeed? Explain your answer. (RA2)

67. Andy feels like his parents don't know much about him and don't understand him at all. How would you describe your relationship with your parents? (RA2)

68. Rhonda says that though there are grief counselors at the school, what really helps students deal with the accident is talking with each other in small groups. How do you deal with difficult situations in your life? How do you make sense of things beyond your control? Who do you rely on for support and encouragement? (RA2)

69. Rhonda says she didn't think it was possible for kids her age to die. She admits to assuming they would all come to the reunion and see each other as old men and women. Why do you think it is hard for teenagers to realize some of their peers will die? Is the death of a teenager more difficult for teens to deal with than the death of an older adult? Explain your answer. (RA1)

70. B.J. says, "Was all this done to teach us kids a lesson? Will it stop us from drinkin' and drivin'? Maybe--a few. But the rest will keep on doing it, no matter what." Some people say that in order to really learn something you have to experience it yourself. Others argue that seeing something happening to someone else serves as an effective warning. What do you think? How would you classify most teenagers? How would you classify yourself? (RA1)

71. Andy tries desperately to help his friend out of the car, but has to watch helplessly as he is burned to death, later realizing it was beyond his control. Have you ever tried to help a friend or family member in a serious situation? What happened? Were you able to help? How did you feel in this situation? (RA1)

QUOTATIONS WORKSHEET *Tears of a Tiger*

1. . . . the whole car is in flames, and Rob is still stuck inside, and we can hear him screamin', "Andy! Andy! Help me--Help me--Oh God, please don't let me die like this! Andy!. . ." He screamed what seemed like a long time. Then it was real quiet. . . . That's what I remember--and that's what I'll never be able to forget. (RA1)

2. Was all this done to teach us kids a lesson? Will it stop us from drinkin' and drivin'? Maybe--a few. But the rest will keep on doing it, no matter what. (RA1)

3. Last week I learned that kids my age could die. That was the most frightening moment I ever had. (RA1)

4. One student became a statistic when he lost his life in an accident involving drinking and driving. Usually, statistics don't mean much, but this statistic had a name, a face, a basketball jersey, and friends. Every 18 minutes, every day of the year, someone is killed in a drunk-driving accident. Alcohol-related fatalities are the number one cause of death in teenagers. When will we learn? (RA1)

5. Well, if you really want to know, I wanted to die right after the accident. I wanted it to be me that was dead instead of Rob. (RA1)

6. I coulda controlled the drinkin'. I knew better. We all did. We just never figured it would happen to us. (RA1)

7. It's going to be rough getting over this. Hardly any of us ever knew anybody who had died before. You kinda figure if you're 17, you'll live forever. But Robbie didn't. (RA2)

8. With a five-dollar bill, Andy and the guys bought a six-pack of beer. They ended up buying five dollars worth of death. (RA2)

9. It's easier to just "make do," to get by. I like gettin' good grades, but my friends talk about me if I get called up to the front on Awards Day with all the white kids. It's easier to sit in the back of the auditorium, and laugh, and make hootin' noises when people like Mary Alice Applesauce go up to get their Honor Roll awards.(RA2)

10. Like the lady said in the poem--you mindin' your own black business and all this white stuff jus' takes over your life. And I ain't jus' talkin' 'bout snow!(RA3)

11. It's society that implants positives or negatives onto certain ideas. You have the option to accept, reject, or change the stereotypes that currently exist. (RA3)

12. It seems like bein' dead is the only way I'll ever feel alive again. (RA4)

13. I will always treasure those days, and I will never forgive myself for destroying something very special. (RA4)

14. I appreciate your efforts, but I feel that you might be overly concerned about a situation that is under control. (RA5)

15. You know what? Just between the two of us, I don't think that accident affected him that much. Black kids are tough. (RA5)

16. He's got his parents, his teachers, even that stupid counselor at the Outpatient Psych Center fooled. They all say stuff like, "Andy sure is adjusting well," because he's smiling and cheerful. (RA5)

17. I wish you'd quit callin' it "the unfortunate incident"! It wasn't an "incident"! It was a crash! A terrible, terrible crash! And it was my fault! You need a dose of reality, Mom. You want to pretend it didn't happen and I can't deal with this by myself. (RA5)

18. It was dark, so I couldn't see, and I was under the water, so I couldn't breathe. I tried to scream, but water got into my mouth and my throat and my chest. I was cryin' out for help, but my cries only made things worse. That's how I feel tonight, Mom. That's *exactly* how I feel tonight. (RA5)

19. [Andy's Father] "Andrew, I know the accident was very traumatic for you. But you have to get beyond it and move on. You have to be strong and show that you are bigger than the problem." [Andy] "Yes, I know. You've told me that before. Be a man. Be strong. Put this 'unfortunate incident' behind you. Well, maybe I can't do that." (RA6)

20. Nobody's home. Nobody cares. Maybe I'll try to sleep. I wish I could sleep forever. (RA6)

21. It's not that I want to die--it's just that I can't stand the pain of livin' anymore. I just want the hurt and pain inside to go away. It's like a monster in my gut--eatin' me up from the inside out. Actually, I feel like the only thing that's keepin' me from going crazy is this terrible, terrible pain. (RA6)

22. Do you know that the courage it took at that moment--to actually blow yourself away--was more than enough courage to keep on living? (RA6)

23. So, I guess the pain is over for you now. You have moved to the place where there is no pain, and I guess that's good. But the pain left by your absence is like a wound in our hearts that will not heal. Nobody understands why you decided to end your life when you had so much to live for. So you're out of it and we have to stay here, feeling your pain as well as our own. It really isn't fair, you know. (RA6)

24. If you slept with a warrior space soldier, maybe you wouldn't have nightmares either. (RA4)

25. She doesn't understand that this time there's no one to pull me out. . . . (RA5)

26. *No son of mine is going to be a failure!* Do you hear me? (RA6)

LESSON SEVENTEEN

Objectives
    1. To discuss the novel on a deeper than direct-recall level
    2. To prepare students for questions and topics covered on the test
    3. To allow students to make personal connection with the text
    4. To allow students to practice writing a letter
    5. To allow students to show the author their appreciation for the book

Activity #1
Continue working on the Extra Discussion Questions as previously described.

Activity #2
Give students the Letter to the Author assignment sheet. If needed, review how to write a formal letter with your students. Give them the remainder of the class time to complete the letter. Once you have proofread all the letters and students have had the chance to correct any mistakes, mail the letters to Sharon Draper at:

Sharon Draper
PO Box 36551
Cincinnati, OH 45236

Sharon Draper states on her website that she will usually write back, but that a class set of letters with a cover letter about your class is the easiest way for her to manage. She would prefer the letters not be mailed individually so she can write a response back to your class to post and share with students.

Note: This assignment may be used as an extra credit opportunity. You may offer extra credit for simply writing the letter, or offer extra credit for those who type their letters.

Letter to the Author

            Often times, books are written to make people think about serious issues. Think about the point the author was trying to make in writing this book. Then, compose a letter to the author expressing how this book has affected your life.

Topics to include in your letter:
- What you liked about the book
- How you could relate to this book
- How realistic the book was
- What you learned from the book
- What issues the book made you think about
- How you felt when reading the book
- How you have changed since reading the book
- Anything else you think the author should know

Necessary Elements:
- Your letter must by typed
- You should begin your letter by saying Dear Ms. _____,
- You should have an introductory paragraph where you introduce yourself
- You should have body paragraphs
- You should have a friendly conclusion to the letter
- Underneath your signature you should include your home address and email address in case the author wishes to write you back

    Remember to proofread this letter and turn it in to me free of errors. I will grade your letter, allow you to make any changes that are needed, and then I will mail your letters to the author of your book. Most authors enjoy receiving letters from readers and like to see how their hard work has affected others. Some authors even respond to letters from their readers, so don't be surprised if you get a reply.

LESSON EIGHTEEN

Objectives
1. To practice speaking and presentation skills
2. To generate class discussion about the unit
3. To connect ideas from the novel with events in students' lives and the lives of those around them
4. To evaluate students' reactions to the unit

Activity #1
Have students present their projects to the class. Ask students to display their projects and share some of the facts they found in their research. If at all possible, allow for discussion of these facts and statistics during presentations. Encourage students to think about the research they did and how it relates to their lives.

Activity #2
Give students the *Tears of a Tiger* Unit Reaction sheet. Give them time to answer the questions and to give feedback about the unit. Read over the feedback and make any necessary adjustments to the unit before you begin to teach it the following year.

UNIT REACTION - *Tears of a Tiger*

1. What were your overall impressions of *Tears of a Tiger*?

2. How likely are you to read one of Sharon Draper's other books?

3. How likely are you to read other young adult books?

4. What was your favorite assignment in the unit? Why?

5. What was your least favorite assignment in the unit? Why?

6. What was most helpful to you in this unit?

7. What assignment do you think should be changed? Why?

8. What was something that surprised you about your topic while doing research?

9. How did the research and information in the projects presented affect you?

10. How has this book and project affected your life (the decisions you make, how you view others, etc)?

Use the space below to write any other comments you have regarding this unit:

LESSON NINETEEN

<u>Objectives</u>
    1. To practice writing to persuade
    2. To improve students' writing abilities
    3. To have students think through what they could do for friends who may need their help

<u>Activity #1</u>
After the project presentations students should now be familiar with a wide variety of teen issues discussed in the novel. The purpose of this writing assignment is to give students the opportunity to write to persuade a friend dealing with one of these problems to get help. Distribute Writing Assignment 3 to your students and use the following rubric to provide feedback.

Note: As students complete this writing assignment, call individuals up for writing conferences on the past two writing assignments. Use the evaluation form to guide you in your conference.

WRITING ASSIGNMENT #3 *Tears of a Tiger*

PROMPT
In the novel you encountered many serious issues that teens were forced to deal with. Through your project, guest speakers, and classroom assignments you learned more about the severity of these issues and the number of teens who deal with them in their lives. Your assignment is to write a letter to persuade a close friend dealing with one of these issues to get the help he or she needs.

PREWRITING
Think about the serious issues that are discussed in the novel (depression, suicide, physical abuse, racial stereotyping, drinking and driving, etc). Select one of these issues to cover in your letter. Using your notes/information from your project and classroom activities, create a list of reasons why your friend should get help. Next, come up with a variety of ways this friend can go about finding help for his or her problem.

DRAFTING
Write an introductory paragraph that addresses your friend and his or her problem. Express your concern for his or her well being and begin to explain why he or she needs to get help.

In the body paragraphs, continue to outline your reasons for wanting your friend to get help. Remember to use your facts, statistics, and examples from the text to support your view. Make each new reason a separate paragraph. After you have outlined the reasons why your friend should stop, offer suggestions on how to get help.

In your conclusion paragraph, make your final plea to your friend. Try to be supportive and sympathetic, while using a strong fact or example to leave the reader with a powerful ending.

PROMPT
When you finish the rough draft of your composition, ask a student who sits near you to read it.

After reading your rough draft, he/she should tell you what he/she liked best about your work, which parts were difficult to understand, and ways in which your work could be improved. Reread your paper considering your critic's comments, and make the corrections you think are necessary. Ask your classmate what he/she thought of each of the characters/events you chose for your assignment.

PROOFREADING
Do a final proofreading of your paper double-checking your grammar, spelling, organization, and the clarity of your ideas.

WRITING EVALUATION FORM - *Tears of a Tiger*

Name _____ Date _____ Writing Assignment # _____

Grade _____

Circle One For Each Item:

Introduction:	excellent	good	fair	poor
Body Paragraphs:	excellent	good	fair	poor
Conclusion:	excellent	good	fair	poor
Grammar:	excellent	good	fair	poor
Spelling:	excellent	good	fair	poor
Punctuation:	excellent	good	fair	poor
Legibility:	excellent	good	fair	poor
_____:	excellent	good	fair	poor
_____:	excellent	good	fair	poor

Strengths:

Weaknesses:

Comments/Suggestions:

LESSON TWENTY

Objectives
To review all of the vocabulary work done in this unit

Activity #1
Choose one (or more) of the vocabulary review activities listed below and spend your class period as directed in the activity. Some of the materials for these review activities are located in the Vocabulary Resource Materials section in this LitPlan.

VOCABULARY REVIEW ACTIVITIES

1. Divide your class into two teams and have an old-fashioned spelling or definition bee.

2. Give each of your students (or students in groups of two, three or four) a *Tears of a Tiger* Vocabulary Word Search Puzzle. The person (group) to find all of the vocabulary words in the puzzle first wins.

3. Give students a *Tears of a Tiger* Vocabulary Word Search Puzzle without the word list. The person or group to find the most vocabulary words in the puzzle wins.

4. Use a *Tears of a Tiger* Vocabulary Crossword Puzzle. Put the puzzle onto a transparency on the overhead projector (so everyone can see it), and do the puzzle together as a class.

5. Give students a *Tears of a Tiger* Vocabulary Matching Worksheet to do.

6. Divide your class into two teams. Use *Tears of a Tiger* vocabulary words with their letters jumbled as a word list. Student 1 from Team A faces off against Student 1 from Team B. You write the first jumbled word on the board. The first student (1A or 1B) to unscramble the word wins the chance for his/her team to score points. If 1A wins the jumble, go to student 2A and give him/her a definition. He/she must give you the correct spelling of the vocabulary word which fits that definition. If he/she does, Team A scores a point, and you give student 3A a definition for which you expect a correctly spelled matching vocabulary word. Continue giving Team A definitions until some team member makes an incorrect response. An incorrect response sends the game back to the jumbled-word face off, this time with students 2A and 2B. Instead of repeating giving definitions to the first few students of each team, continue with the student after the one who gave the last incorrect response on the team. For example, if Team B wins the jumbled-word face-off, and student 5B gave the last incorrect answer for Team B, you would start this round of definition questions with student 6B, and so on. The team with the most points wins!

7. Have students write a story in which they correctly use as many vocabulary words as possible. Have students read their compositions orally! Post the most original compositions on your bulletin board!

LESSON TWENTY ONE

Objectives
To review the main ideas and events in *Tears of a Tiger*

Activity #1
Choose one of the review games/activities suggested in this unit and spend your class time as directed there.

REVIEW GAMES/ACTIVITIES

1. Ask the class to make up a unit test for *Tears of a Tiger*. The test should have 4 sections: matching, true/false, short answer, and essay. Students may use 1/2 period to make the test and then swap papers and use the other 1/2 class period to take a test a classmate has devised. (open book) You may want to use the unit test included in this packet or take questions from the students' unit tests to formulate your own test.

2. Take 1/2 period for students to make up true and false questions (including the answers). Collect the papers and divide the class into two teams. Draw a big tic-tac-toe board on the chalk board. Make one team X and one team O. Ask questions to each side, giving each student one turn. If the question is answered correctly, that students' team's letter (X or O) is placed in the box. If the answer is incorrect, no letter is placed in the box. The object is to get three in a row like tic-tac-toe. You may want to keep track of the number of games won for each team.

3. Take 1/2 period for students to make up questions (true/false and short answer). Collect the questions. Divide the class into two teams. You'll alternate asking questions to individual members of teams A & B (like in a spelling bee). The question keeps going from A to B until it is correctly answered, then a new question is asked. A correct answer does not allow the team to get another question. Correct answers are +2 points; incorrect answers are -1 point.

4. Have students pair up and quiz each other from their study guides and class notes.

5. Give students a *Tears of a Tiger* crossword puzzle to complete.

6. Play What's My Line?. This is similar to the old television show. Students assume the roles of different characters from the story. One student gives clues to the class, or to a panel of contestants. The contestants try to guess the identity of the guest. Students may enjoy assisting you in creating rules and procedures for the game.

7. Divide your class into two teams. Use *Tears of a Tiger* crossword words with their letters jumbled as a word list. Student 1 from Team A faces off against Student 1 from Team B. You write the first jumbled word on the board. The first student (1A or 1B) to unscramble the word wins the chance for his/her team to score points. If 1A wins the jumble, go to student 2A and give him/her a clue. He/she must give you the correct word which matches that clue. If he/she does, Team A scores a point, and you give student 3A a clue for which you expect another correct response. Continue giving Team A clues until some team member makes an incorrect response. An incorrect response sends the game back to the jumbled-word face off, this time with students 2A and 2B. Instead of repeating giving clues to the first few students of each team, continue with the student after the one who gave the last incorrect response on the team. For example, if Team B wins the jumbled-word face-off, and student 5B gave the last incorrect answer for Team B, you would start this round of clue questions with student 6B, and so on. The team with the most points wins!

8. Play Jeopardy. Divide the class into two groups. Assign each group a category from the story and have them devise answers for that category. Play the game according to the television show procedures.

9. Play Drawing in the Details. This is similar to Pictionary. Divide students into teams. A student from one team draws a scene from the story. (You may want to specify the Book or section.) Drawings should be kept simple, to keep the pace lively. Students in the opposing team locate the scene in their books and read it aloud. If they are incorrect, the illustrator's team has a chance to guess. Involve students in setting up a scoring system and any other necessary rules.

LESSON TWENTY TWO

Objectives
To test the students' understanding of the main ideas and themes in *Tears of a Tiger*

Activity #1
Distribute the unit tests. Go over the instructions in detail and allow the students the entire class period to complete the exam.

NOTES ABOUT THE UNIT TESTS IN THIS UNIT:

There are 5 different unit tests included in the LitPlan Teacher Pack. Two are short answer, two are multiple choice. There is one advanced short answer test. The answers to the advanced short answer test will be based on the discussions you have had during class and should be graded accordingly. You should choose the tests and/or test parts which best suit your needs. Matching and short answer tests have answer keys. For essay type questions, grade according to your own criteria based on class discussions and the level of your students. Also, you will need to choose vocabulary words to read orally for the vocabulary section of the short answer tests.

Activity #2
Collect all test papers and assigned books prior to the end of the class period.

UNIT TESTS

Tears of a Tiger SHORT ANSWER UNIT TEST 1

I. MATCHING

____ 1. ALCOHOL   A. Keisha's best friend

____ 2. GERALD   B. Invited but decides not to go out with the boys after the game

____ 3. TYRONE   C. Even though Andy writes this, he doesn't turn it in for a grade.

____ 4. BJ   D. Carrothers

____ 5. KEISHA   E. Gerald would get rid of peanut butter, these, and $5 bills.

____ 6. POEM   F. B.J. and Tyrone go to see this person in hopes of helping Andy.

____ 7. LETTER   G. Keisha says life without them would be boring and meaningless.

____ 8. COUNSELOR   H. The only one not drinking the night of the accident

____ 9. PSYCHOLOGIST   I. What Andy's dad always calls his son

____ 10. RHONDA   J. Keisha is bored with Andy's depression & her mom picks her up there.

____ 11. SCOUTS   K. Monty visits Andy there.

____ 12. ANDREW   L. The cause of the car accident

____ 13. MONTY   M. Andy thinks she loves him.

____ 14. BANDAIDS   N. Helped Andy out of the car

____ 15. FRIENDS   O. Andy's little brother

____ 16. GRAVE   P. Andy sends this to Rob's parents at his psychologist's request.

____ 17. JEFFERSON   Q. Coach who tried to help Andy

____ 18. MALL   R. Andy's last name

____ 19. MOVIES   S. Keisha is too busy to go there with Andy.

____ 20. RIPLEY   T. They were looking for Andy, but he wasn't at school.

II. SHORT ANSWER

1. B.J. was the only one not drinking on the night of the accident. Later, he feels guilty and wonders if he should have stopped them from driving or offered to drive. What reason does he give for not speaking up?

2. How does Andy describe his relationship with his family to his psychologist?

3. Andy tells Dr. Carrothers that Keisha is there for him when no one else is. What examples does he give to show that she is "there for him"?

4. What does Andy say in his letter to Rob's parents?

5. What does Andy say to Dr. Carrothers to convince the doctor that he has improved enough to have appointments on an as-needed basis?

6. How does Andy's mother respond when Andy asks for help handling the accident?

7. Which three people does Andy try to call before he kills himself, and what response does he get from each?

8. What does Monty see on the ceiling?

9. Why is Tyrone mad at the suicide prevention/grief counseling woman at their school?

10. What does the grief counselor suggest Andy's friends should do to try to work through their pain and frustration over Andy's death?

III. QUOTATIONS: Explain the importance and meaning of the following quotations:

1. Was all this done to teach us kids a lesson? Will it stop us from drinkin' and drivin'? Maybe--a few. But the rest will keep on doing it, no matter what. (RA1)

2. It's society that implants positives or negatives onto certain ideas. You have the option to accept, reject, or change the stereotypes that currently exist. (RA3)

3. He's got his parents, his teachers, even that stupid counselor at the Outpatient Psych Center fooled. They all say stuff like, "Andy sure is adjusting well," because he's smiling and cheerful. (RA5)

4. It was dark, so I couldn't see, and I was under the water, so I couldn't breathe. I tried to scream, but water got into my mouth and my throat and my chest. I was cryin' out for help, but my cries only made things worse. That's how I feel tonight, Mom. That's *exactly* how I feel tonight. (RA5)

5. Do you know that the courage it took at that moment--to actually blow yourself away--was more than enough courage to keep on living? (RA6)

IV. COMPOSITION

1. B.J. is angry because Andy didn't ask for help before killing himself. Is this true? Explain your answer. (RA6)

2. What is the significance of the title? (ALL)

V. Vocabulary
A. Write the vocabulary words you are given. After writing them down, go back and write in their definitions.

Word	Definition
1	
2	
3	
4	
5	
6	
7	
8	
9	
10	

Tears of a Tiger SHORT ANSWER UNIT TEST 1 Answer Key

I. MATCHING

L	1. ALCOHOL	A. Keisha's best friend
B	2. GERALD	B. Invited but decides not to go out with the boys after the game
N	3. TYRONE	C. Even though Andy writes this, he doesn't turn it in for a grade.
H	4. BJ	D. Carrothers
M	5. KEISHA	E. Gerald would get rid of peanut butter, these, and $5 bills.
C	6. POEM	F. B.J. and Tyrone go to see this person in hopes of helping Andy.
P	7. LETTER	G. Keisha says life without them would be boring and meaningless.
F	8. COUNSELOR	H. The only one not drinking the night of the accident
D	9. PSYCHOLOGIST	I. What Andy's dad always calls his son
A	10. RHONDA	J. Keisha is bored with Andy's depression & her mom picks her up there.
T	11. SCOUTS	K. Monty visits Andy there.
I	12. ANDREW	L. The cause of the car accident
O	13. MONTY	M. Andy thinks she loves him.
E	14. BANDAIDS	N. Helped Andy out of the car
G	15. FRIENDS	O. Andy's little brother
K	16. GRAVE	P. Andy sends this to Rob's parents at his psychologist's request.
R	17. JEFFERSON	Q. Coach who tried to help Andy
J	18. MALL	R. Andy's last name
S	19. MOVIES	S. Keisha is too busy to go there with Andy.
Q	20. RIPLEY	T. They were looking for Andy, but he wasn't at school.

II. SHORT ANSWER

1. B.J. was the only one not drinking on the night of the accident. Later, he feels guilty and wonders if he should have stopped them from driving or offered to drive. What reason does he give for not speaking up?
   B.J. feels lucky to hang out with the other boys since he is not very popular and is the only one of the group not on the basketball team. He admits he is usually so happy to be invited out with the guys that he doesn't try to change what they are doing.

2. How does Andy describe his relationship with his family to his psychologist?
   Andy says his parents don't understand him at all. His father works all the time and his mother is out of touch with reality. Andy feels like they love his younger brother more than him.

3. Andy tells Dr. Carrothers that Keisha is there for him when no one else is. What examples does he give to show that she is "there for him"?
   Keisha came to the hospital, the funeral, and the trial to support Andy. She is also the only person he feels like he can cry in front of, and when he does, she comforts him. Andy says he can always call her, and she will cheer him up.

4. What does Andy say in his letter to Rob's parents?
   Andy asks for forgiveness, but says he understands if they cannot give it. He then makes a list of all the good things he remembers about Rob to help Rob's parents focus on the good memories instead of the bad reality.

5. What does Andy say to Dr. Carrothers to convince the doctor that he has improved enough to have appointments on an as-needed basis?
   Andy says he's sleeping better and doing better in school. He admits he still blames himself but also says he is learning to live with the guilt. He says he has his act together and no longer needs to come to therapy.

6. How does Andy's mother respond when Andy asks for help handling the accident? *She tells him that time will heal all wounds and that he's young and resilient so he will bounce back.*

7. Which three people does Andy try to call before he kills himself, and what response does he get from each?
   Andy calls Dr. Carrothers, who is out of town and cannot take the call, Keisha, whose mother answers and says she is asleep, and his basketball coach, who is not home.

8. What does Monty see on the ceiling?
   Andy's little brother Monty notices blood on the ceiling when he and his mother get home.

9. Why is Tyrone mad at the suicide prevention/grief counseling woman at their school? *Tyrone is angry because he and B.J. went to the school counselor with their concerns about Andy and his depression, but no one did anything until it was too late. He wonders where the suicide posters and hotline numbers were last week when Andy was about to kill himself.*

10. What does the grief counselor suggest Andy's friends should do to try to work through their pain and frustration over Andy's death?
    She recommends they each write a letter to Andy explaining how they feel.

V. Vocabulary
    Write the vocabulary words and definitions you will use for this test.

Word	Definition
1	
2	
3	
4	
5	
6	
7	
8	
9	
10	

Tears of a Tiger SHORT ANSWER UNIT TEST 2

I. MATCHING

____ 1. GERALD   A. ___'s home. ___ cares....I wish I could sleep forever.

____ 2. TYRONE   B. No son of mine is going to be a ___!

____ 3. BJ   C. Andy's little brother

____ 4. LAW   D. What Andy says he sees in his future

____ 5. KEISHA   E. Andy thinks she loves him.

____ 6. ROCK   F. I knew better. We all did. We just never figured it would happen to __.

____ 7. NOTHING   G. Rhonda's most frightening moment: realizing that kids could ___

____ 8. COUNSELOR   H. The only one not drinking the night of the accident

____ 9. PSYCHOLOGIST   I. Andy's father brushes off her concerns.

____ 10. RHONDA   J. Andy may want to major in this.

____ 11. TEACHER   K. Carrothers

____ 12. TIGER   L. Rob's last name

____ 13. MONTY   M. Keisha's best friend

____ 14. PRAY   N. Helped Andy out of the car

____ 15. MACBETH   O. BJ does this to help cope with the accident.

____ 16. DIE   P. B.J. and Tyrone go to see this person in hopes of helping Andy.

____ 17. FAILURE   Q. Invited but decides not to go out with the boys after the game

____ 18. WASHINGTON   R. What Rob's mother would always tell Andy he got for Christmas

____ 19. NOBODY   S. Story Andy's class is reading when he runs out of the classroom.

____ 20. US   T. Monty puts tears on this animal.

II. SHORT ANSWER

1. How does Andy's personality change following the accident? What do his friends begin to notice about him?

2. How does Andy describe his relationship with his family to his psychologist?

3. Why does Andy choose to let his grades slide?

4. What promise does Dr. Carrothers make Andy agree to during their therapy session?

5. When B.J. and Tyrone are concerned about Andy and go to talk to the school counselor about him, what is her response to their concerns?

6. Andy talks to his mother after the talent show, to try to explain to her how he feels. To what does he compare his feelings?

7. Which three people does Andy try to call before he kills himself, and what response does he get from each?

8. What does Monty see on the ceiling?

9. Why is Tyrone mad at the suicide prevention/grief counseling woman at their school?

10. How do each of Andy's friends react to his suicide?

III. QUOTATIONS: Explain the importance and meaning of the following quotations:

1. Last week I learned that kids my age could die. That was the most frightening moment I ever had. (RA1)

2. I coulda controlled the drinkin'. I knew better. We all did. We just never figured it would happen to us. (RA1)

3. Like the lady said in the poem--you mindin' your own black business and all this white stuff jus' takes over your life. And I ain't jus' talkin' 'bout snow!(RA3)

4. [Andy's Father] "Andrew, I know the accident was very traumatic for you. But you have to get beyond it and move on. You have to be strong and show that you are bigger than the problem." [Andy] "Yes, I know. You've told me that before. Be a man. Be strong. Put this 'unfortunate incident' behind you. Well, maybe I can't do that." (RA6)

5. So, I guess the pain is over for you now. You have moved to the place where there is no pain, and I guess that's good. But the pain left by your absence is like a wound in our hearts that will not heal. Nobody understands why you decided to end your life when you had so much to live for. So you're out of it and we have to stay here, feeling your pain as well as our own. It really isn't fair, you know. (RA6)

IV. COMPOSITION
1. What is the significance of the title? (ALL)

2. How does the point of view enhance the novel? Give specific examples to support your answer. (ALL)

V. Vocabulary

A. Write the vocabulary words you are given. After writing them down, go back and write in their definitions.

Word	Definition
1	
2	
3	
4	
5	
6	
7	
8	
9	
10	

Tears of a Tiger SHORT ANSWER UNIT TEST 2 Answer Key

I. MATCHING

Q	1. GERALD	A. ___'s home. ___ cares....I wish I could sleep forever.
N	2. TYRONE	B. No son of mine is going to be a ___!
H	3. BJ	C. Andy's little brother
J	4. LAW	D. What Andy says he sees in his future
E	5. KEISHA	E. Andy thinks she loves him.
R	6. ROCK	F. I knew better. We all did. We just never figured it would happen to __.
D	7. NOTHING	G. Rhonda's most frightening moment: realizing that kids could ___
P	8. COUNSELOR	H. The only one not drinking the night of the accident
K	9. PSYCHOLOGIST	I. Andy's father brushes off her concerns.
M	10. RHONDA	J. Andy may want to major in this.
I	11. TEACHER	K. Carrothers
T	12. TIGER	L. Rob's last name
C	13. MONTY	M. Keisha's best friend
O	14. PRAY	N. Helped Andy out of the car
S	15. MACBETH	O. BJ does this to help cope with the accident.
G	16. DIE	P. B.J. and Tyrone go to see this person in hopes of helping Andy.
B	17. FAILURE	Q. Invited but decides not to go out with the boys after the game
L	18. WASHINGTON	R. What Rob's mother would always tell Andy he got for Christmas
A	19. NOBODY	S. Story Andy's class is reading when he runs out of the classroom.
F	20. US	T. Monty puts tears on this animal.

II. SHORT ANSWER

1. How does Andy's personality change following the accident? What do his friends begin to notice about him?
   Andy likes to be alone a lot, and he has crying spells. They also say he is depressed.

2. How does Andy describe his relationship with his family to his psychologist?
   Andy says his parents don't understand him at all. His father works all the time and his mother is out of touch with reality. Andy feels like they love his younger brother more than him.

3. Why does Andy choose to let his grades slide?
   Andy gives several reasons why he lets his grades slide. He says his parents push him to be something he isn't, his friends make fun of him if he does well, his counselor doesn't believe he will be able to be anything but an athlete, and his teachers set very low expectations for black students.

4. What promise does Dr. Carrothers make Andy agree to during their therapy session? *Dr. Carrothers makes Andy promise that if he ever gets too depressed he will call him before he tries to hurt himself.*

5. When B.J. and Tyrone are concerned about Andy and go to talk to the school counselor about him, what is her response to their concerns?
   She tells the boys Andy is getting counseling outside of school and not to worry, he's getting the help he needs.

6. Andy talks to his mother after the talent show, to try to explain to her how he feels. To what does he compare his feelings?
   Andy tells her a story of when he was nine and fell into a tide pool late at night. He was under water and couldn't breathe, and he was crying for help but it only made things worse. Andy tries to tell her that's how he feels now and that he can't handle this all by himself.

7. Which three people does Andy try to call before he kills himself, and what response does he get from each?
   Andy calls Dr. Carrothers, who is out of town and cannot take the call, Keisha, whose mother answers and says she is asleep, and his basketball coach, who is not home.

8. What does Monty see on the ceiling?
   Andy's little brother Monty notices blood on the ceiling when he and his mother get home.

9. Why is Tyrone mad at the suicide prevention/grief counseling woman at their school? *Tyrone is angry because he and B.J. went to the school counselor with their concerns about Andy and his depression, but no one did anything until it was too late. He wonders where the suicide posters and hotline numbers were last week when Andy was about to kill himself.*

10. How do each of Andy's friends react to his suicide?
    Tyrone: Says he will never understand why Andy did it and thinks Andy should have valued life more; very angry at Andy for what he did Gerald: Is very mad at Andy and says he was a coward; says he hates Andy for doing this
    Marcus: Says he always wanted to be like Andy but feels better about who he is since he never knew the pain Andy was going through
    Rhonda: Is mad Andy didn't think about his family or friends finding his body or dealing with his suicide
    Keisha: Shocked that Andy is actually dead and is upset that she has to stay behind and deal with the pain he caused
    B.J.: Prays to God to watch over Andy and help him find peace

V. Vocabulary

Write the vocabulary words and definitions you will use for this test.

Word	Definition
1	
2	
3	
4	
5	
6	
7	
8	
9	
10	

Tears of a Tiger ADVANCED SHORT ANSWER UNIT TEST

I. MATCHING

____ 1. GERALD   A. Carrothers

____ 2. TYRONE   B. Andy thinks she loves him.

____ 3. BJ   C. Andy gets this position on the team after Rob's death.

____ 4. CAPTAIN   D. Keisha says life without them would be boring and meaningless.

____ 5. HOMICIDE   E. Topic of discussion after reading the poem about snow

____ 6. KEISHA   F. Andy sends this to Rob's parents at his psychologist's request.

____ 7. POEM   G. Helped Andy out of the car

____ 8. RACE   H. ___'s home. ___ cares....I wish I could sleep forever.

____ 9. LETTER   I.   Andy's friends think he is a _____ for killing himself.

____ 10. COUNSELOR   J. Andy's little brother

____ 11. PSYCHOLOGIST   K. Even though Andy writes this, he doesn't turn it in for a grade.

____ 12. RHONDA   L. B.J. and Tyrone go to see this person in hopes of helping Andy.

____ 13. TALENT   M. Gerald is a victim of this.

____ 14. DROWNED   N. Andy is charged with DWI and vehicular _____.

____ 15. CEILING   O. The only one not drinking the night of the accident

____ 16. MONTY   P. Keisha and Andy break up at the _____ show.

____ 17. COWARD   Q. Keisha's best friend

____ 18. ABUSE   R. Andy tells his mother about a time when he was younger and almost _____.

____ 19. FRIENDS   S. Monty wonders why there is blood on this.

____ 20. NOBODY   T. Invited but decides not to go out with the boys after the game

II. SHORT ANSWER

1. B.J. feels guilty and has trouble understanding why Rob had to die. What reasons does he have to feel guilty? Do you think he is justified in feeling guilty? Explain why or why not. (RA1)

2. What can readers infer about Andy's relationship with his parents? Use details from the text to support your answer. (RA2)

3. Analyze the poem Andy writes for his English class. What does this reveal about what he's feeling? Knowing the poem is worth a large portion of his grade, why doesn't he turn it in? (RA3)

4. Andy describes several instances when he is the victim of stereotyping due to his skin color. How does he deal with these feelings? How does this affect him? (RA3)

5. Compare and contrast how B.J. and Tyrone deal with the accident with how Andy deals with the accident. (RA4)

6. B.J. is angry because Andy didn't ask for help before killing himself. Is this true? Explain your answer. (RA6)

7. Andy's friends are shocked that he killed himself. Did you predict that Andy would kill himself at the end of the novel? What clues did the author provide to let you know that Andy was going to do something drastic? (RA6)

8. What is the significance of the title? (ALL)

9. How does the point of view enhance the novel? Give specific examples to support your answer. (ALL)

10. Andy feels like he deserved a tougher sentence in court. Why does he feel this way? Why does the judge give him a lighter sentence? Would a tougher sentence have made a difference in the outcome for Andy?

III. QUOTATIONS: Explain the importance and meaning of the following quotations:

1. Was all this done to teach us kids a lesson? Will it stop us from drinkin' and drivin'? Maybe--a few. But the rest will keep on doing it, no matter what. (RA1)

2. Like the lady said in the poem--you mindin' your own black business and all this white stuff jus' takes over your life. And I ain't jus' talkin' 'bout snow!(RA3)

3. It's society that implants positives or negatives onto certain ideas. You have the option to accept, reject, or change the stereotypes that currently exist. (RA3)

4. I appreciate your efforts, but I feel that you might be overly concerned about a situation that is under control. (RA5)

5. He's got his parents, his teachers, even that stupid counselor at the Outpatient Psych Center fooled. They all say stuff like, "Andy sure is adjusting well," because he's smiling and cheerful. (RA5)

6. It was dark, so I couldn't see, and I was under the water, so I couldn't breathe. I tried to scream, but water got into my mouth and my throat and my chest. I was cryin' out for help, but my cries only made things worse. That's how I feel tonight, Mom. That's *exactly* how I feel tonight. (RA5)

7. [Andy's Father] "Andrew, I know the accident was very traumatic for you. But you have to get beyond it and move on. You have to be strong and show that you are bigger than the problem." [Andy] "Yes, I know. You've told me that before. Be a man. Be strong. Put this 'unfortunate incident' behind you. Well, maybe I can't do that." (RA6)

8. Do you know that the courage it took at that moment--to actually blow yourself away--was more than enough courage to keep on living? (RA6)

IV. COMPOSITION
1. How was each character changed by the events in the novel? List 4 main characters and briefly tell how each was affected. (ALL)

2. What are the main themes of the novel? Briefly describe each. (ALL)

V. Vocabulary

A. Write the vocabulary words you are given. After writing them down, go back and write in their definitions.

Word	Definition
1	
2	
3	
4	
5	
6	
7	
8	
9	
10	

B. Write a paragraph about the book using 8 of the 10 vocabulary words above.

Tears of a Tiger ADVANCED SHORT ANSWER UNIT TEST Answer Key

I. MATCHING

T	1. GERALD	A. Carrothers
G	2. TYRONE	B. Andy thinks she loves him.
O	3. BJ	C. Andy gets this position on the team after Rob's death.
C	4. CAPTAIN	D. Keisha says life without them would be boring and meaningless.
N	5. HOMICIDE	E. Topic of discussion after reading the poem about snow
B	6. KEISHA	F. Andy sends this to Rob's parents at his psychologist's request.
K	7. POEM	G. Helped Andy out of the car
E	8. RACE	H. ___'s home. ___ cares....I wish I could sleep forever.
F	9. LETTER	I. Andy's friends think he is a _____ for killing himself.
L	10. COUNSELOR	J. Andy's little brother
A	11. PSYCHOLOGIST	K. Even though Andy writes this, he doesn't turn it in for a grade.
Q	12. RHONDA	L. B.J. and Tyrone go to see this person in hopes of helping Andy.
P	13. TALENT	M. Gerald is a victim of this.
R	14. DROWNED	N. Andy is charged with DWI and vehicular _____.
S	15. CEILING	O. The only one not drinking the night of the accident
J	16. MONTY	P. Keisha and Andy break up at the _____ show.
I	17. COWARD	Q. Keisha's best friend
M	18. ABUSE	R. Andy tells his mother about a time when he was younger and almost _____.
D	19. FRIENDS	S. Monty wonders why there is blood on this.
H	20. NOBODY	T. Invited but decides not to go out with the boys after the game

V. Vocabulary
   Write the vocabulary words and definitions you will use for this test.

	Word	Definition
1		
2		
3		
4		
5		
6		
7		
8		
9		
10		

Tears of a Tiger MULTIPLE CHOICE UNIT TEST 1

I. MATCHING

____ 1. ALCOHOL   A. Andy's last name

____ 2. GERALD   B. Carrothers

____ 3. TYRONE   C. Keisha says life without them would be boring and meaningless.

____ 4. BJ   D. Keisha's best friend

____ 5. KEISHA   E. Monty visits Andy there.

____ 6. POEM   F. Keisha is bored with Andy's depression & her mom picks her up there.

____ 7. LETTER   G. Keisha is too busy to go there with Andy.

____ 8. COUNSELOR   H. Even though Andy writes this, he doesn't turn it in for a grade.

____ 9. PSYCHOLOGIST   I. What Andy's dad always calls his son

____ 10. RHONDA   J. They were looking for Andy, but he wasn't at school.

____ 11. SCOUTS   K. Coach who tried to help Andy

____ 12. ANDREW   L. Andy thinks she loves him.

____ 13. MONTY   M. Gerald would get rid of peanut butter, these, and $5 bills.

____ 14. BANDAIDS   N. The cause of the car accident

____ 15. FRIENDS   O. Andy sends this to Rob's parents at his psychologist's request.

____ 16. GRAVE   P. Helped Andy out of the car

____ 17. JEFFERSON   Q. Andy's little brother

____ 18. MALL   R. Invited but decides not to go out with the boys after the game

____ 19. MOVIES   S. The only one not drinking the night of the accident

____ 20. RIPLEY   T. B.J. and Tyrone go to see this person in hopes of helping Andy.

II. MULTIPLE CHOICE

1. B.J. was the only one not drinking on the night of the accident. Later, he feels guilty and wonders if he should have stopped them from driving or offered to drive. What reason does he give for not speaking up?

    A. He knows the guys would have made fun of him.

    B. He has tried to stop them before but knows they never listen.

    C. He feels lucky to hang out with them, so he never tries to change their plans.

    D. He worries they will get angry and leave him on the side of the road.

2. How does Andy describe his relationship with his family to his psychologist?

    A. He says his parents are hard on him sometimes, but he knows it's because they love him. His father wants him to go to college and his mother encourages him to do his best in everything. He sometimes feels annoyed and pressured but ultimately knows they love him.

    B. He says his parents are like any other parents. His father gets on his case from time to time, and his mother is very involved in his life. He just feels like any other average teenager with a normal family life.

    C. He says his parents fight all the time and make life hard for him and his brother. His father drinks and takes it out on the family, making his mother depressed. He feels like his home life is tough.

    D. He says his parents don't understand him at all. His father works all the time and his mother is out of touch with reality. He feels like they love his younger brother more than him.

3. Andy tells Dr. Carrothers that Keisha is there for him when no one else is. What examples does he give to show that she is "there for him"?

    A. She came to the hospital, the funeral, and the trial. She is the only person he can cry in front of, and when he does, she comforts him. He also says when he calls her she cheers him up.

    B. She encourages him to write out his feelings in a journal and then talk about them with others. He also says that she is the only person who understands how important therapy is.

    C. She comes over to his house every day so he doesn't have to be alone with his dark thoughts. He also says that she helps keep him organized and prepared for his classes at school.

    D. She goes to the cemetery with him each week to put fresh flowers on Robbie's grave. He also says she is the only one who listens to him.

4. What does Andy say in his letter to Rob's parents?

   A. He tells them he is considering suicide and admits it wasn't even his idea to help Rob.

   B. He admits he bought the beer and includes a photo of Rob from earlier that night.

   C. He asks for forgiveness and makes a list of all the good things he remembers about Rob.

   D. He tells them he is sorry and writes a short poem remembering Rob.

5. What does Andy say to Dr. Carrothers to convince the doctor that he has improved enough to have appointments on an as-needed basis?

   A. He says he's sleeping better and doing better in school. He admits he still blames himself but says that he is learning to live with the guilt.

   B. He says his has stopped thinking about suicide and is a happier person. He says he has forgiven himself and no longer feels guilty.

   C. He says he has improved his relationship with his parents and feels like he can talk to them now. He says he doesn't need a therapist because his parents can help him.

   D. He says his parents can no longer afford private therapy, and he will just talk with the school counselor unless things get bad again.

6. How does Andy's mother respond when Andy asks for help handling the accident?

   A. She tells him she doesn't know any way to help him and that he should talk to his dad.

   B. She tells him it's all her fault and that she should have realized he needed help sooner.

   C. She tells him she will do everything she can to help him, including coming home earlier to spend more time with him.

   D. She tells him that time will heal all wounds and that he's young and resilient so he will bounce back.

7. Which three people does Andy try to call before he kills himself, and what response does he get from each?

   A. He calls Rhonda, who is busy hanging out with Tyrone, Keisha, who is studying, and his coach, who is not at home.

   B. He tries to talk to his mom, who is working on stuff for the homeowners' group, his dad, who is working late at the office, and his brother, who is too young to understand.

   C. He calls Tyrone, who is out on a date with Rhonda, Keisha, who is still mad at him from the talent show, and B.J., who is at church.

   D. He calls Dr. Carrothers, who is out of town and cannot take the call, Keisha, whose mother answers and says she is asleep, and his basketball coach, who is not home.

8. What does Monty see on the ceiling?

    A. A note

    B. Blood

    C. A hole from the shotgun

    D. A noose

9. Why is Tyrone mad at the suicide prevention/grief counseling woman at their school?

    A. He is angry because he and B.J. went to the school counselor with their concerns about Andy and his depression, but no one did anything until it was too late.

    B. He is angry because he called the hotline, and no one ever contacted Andy to see if he was okay until two days after his suicide.

    C. He is angry because she is putting all the blame of Andy's suicide on the student body for not noticing his depression and trying to help.

    D. He is angry because she doesn't know how to help the student body deal with Andy's suicide. All her suggestions don't seem to help anyone feel better about what happened.

10. What does the grief counselor suggest Andy's friends should do to try to work through their pain and frustration over Andy's death?

    A. Attend a grief counseling seminar at the community outreach center

    B. Pray for help is dealing with the pain

    C. Write a letter to Andy explaining how they feel

    D. Share their feelings one at a time while others listen

III. QUOTATIONS: Explain the importance and meaning of the following quotations:

1. Was all this done to teach us kids a lesson? Will it stop us from drinkin' and drivin'? Maybe--a few. But the rest will keep on doing it, no matter what. (RA1)

2. It's society that implants positives or negatives onto certain ideas. You have the option to accept, reject, or change the stereotypes that currently exist. (RA3)

3. He's got his parents, his teachers, even that stupid counselor at the Outpatient Psych Center fooled. They all say stuff like, "Andy sure is adjusting well," because he's smiling and cheerful. (RA5)

4. It was dark, so I couldn't see, and I was under the water, so I couldn't breathe. I tried to scream, but water got into my mouth and my throat and my chest. I was cryin' out for help, but my cries only made things worse. That's how I feel tonight, Mom. That's *exactly* how I feel tonight. (RA5)

5. Do you know that the courage it took at that moment--to actually blow yourself away--was more than enough courage to keep on living? (RA6)

IV. VOCABULARY

____ 1. HONORABLE A. Distrusting or seeing the worst in the motives of others

____ 2. VAST B. Conscious or unconscious restraint of a behavior

____ 3. UNRULY C. Unable to be avoided or escaped; certain

____ 4. TRIBUTE D. Deal out; distribute

____ 5. CAPABLE E. Having ability

____ 6. DISPENSE F. Difficult or impossible to discipline or control

____ 7. RIGHTEOUS G. Actually; really; authentically

____ 8. DENSE H. A cause of loss, damage, disadvantage, or injury

____ 9. COMMODITIES I. Easily perceived or understood

____ 10. CYNICAL J. Very great in area or extent; immense

____ 11. APPARENT K. A useful and desirable thing or quality

____ 12. INEVITABLE L. Articles of trade or commerce; products

____ 13. GENUINELY M. Become a part of the main or dominant culture

____ 14. INHIBITIONS N. Acting in an upright, moral way; virtuous

____ 15. INTENTIONS O. An acknowledgment of gratitude, respect, or admiration

____ 16. REPREHENSIBLE P. Deserving of reproof, rebuke, or censure; blameworthy

____ 17. PUNITIVE Q. Deserving or winning respect or distinction

____ 18. DETRIMENT R. Difficult to understand or follow because of being closely packed with ideas or complexities of style

____ 19. ASSET S. Punishing

____ 20. ASSIMILATE T. Objectives; motives

V. COMPOSITION

1. B.J. is angry because Andy didn't ask for help before killing himself. Is this true? Explain your answer. (RA6)

2. What is the significance of the title? (ALL)

Tears of a Tiger MULTIPLE CHOICE UNIT TEST 1 Answer Key

I. MATCHING

N	1. ALCOHOL	A.	Andy's last name
R	2. GERALD	B.	Carrothers
P	3. TYRONE	C.	Keisha says life without them would be boring and meaningless.
S	4. BJ	D.	Keisha's best friend
L	5. KEISHA	E.	Monty visits Andy there.
H	6. POEM	F.	Keisha is bored with Andy's depression & her mom picks her up there.
O	7. LETTER	G.	Keisha is too busy to go there with Andy.
T	8. COUNSELOR	H.	Even though Andy writes this, he doesn't turn it in for a grade.
B	9. PSYCHOLOGIST	I.	What Andy's dad always calls his son
D	10. RHONDA	J.	They were looking for Andy, but he wasn't at school.
J	11. SCOUTS	K.	Coach who tried to help Andy
I	12. ANDREW	L.	Andy thinks she loves him.
Q	13. MONTY	M.	Gerald would get rid of peanut butter, these, and $5 bills.
M	14. BANDAIDS	N.	The cause of the car accident
C	15. FRIENDS	O.	Andy sends this to Rob's parents at his psychologist's request.
E	16. GRAVE	P.	Helped Andy out of the car
A	17. JEFFERSON	Q.	Andy's little brother
F	18. MALL	R.	Invited but decides not to go out with the boys after the game
G	19. MOVIES	S.	The only one not drinking the night of the accident
K	20. RIPLEY	T.	B.J. and Tyrone go to see this person in hopes of helping Andy.

II. MULTIPLE CHOICE

C 1. B.J. was the only one not drinking on the night of the accident. Later, he feels guilty and wonders if he should have stopped them from driving or offered to drive. What reason does he give for not speaking up?

   A. He knows the guys would have made fun of him.

   B. He has tried to stop them before but knows they never listen.

   C. He feels lucky to hang out with them, so he never tries to change their plans.

   D. He worries they will get angry and leave him on the side of the road.

D 2. How does Andy describe his relationship with his family to his psychologist? A. He says his parents are hard on him sometimes, but he knows it's because they love him. His father wants him to go to college and his mother encourages him to do his best in everything. He sometimes feels annoyed and pressured but ultimately knows they love him.

   B. He says his parents are like any other parents. His father gets on his case from time to time, and his mother is very involved in his life. He just feels like any other average teenager with a normal family life.

   C. He says his parents fight all the time and make life hard for him and his brother. His father drinks and takes it out on the family, making his mother depressed. He feels like his home life is tough.

   D. He says his parents don't understand him at all. His father works all the time and his mother is out of touch with reality. He feels like they love his younger brother more than him.

A 3. Andy tells Dr. Carrothers that Keisha is there for him when no one else is. What examples does he give to show that she is "there for him"?

   A. She came to the hospital, the funeral, and the trial. She is the only person he can cry in front of, and when he does, she comforts him. He also says when he calls her she cheers him up.

   B. She encourages him to write out his feelings in a journal and then talk about them with others. He also says that she is the only person who understands how important therapy is.

   C. She comes over to his house every day so he doesn't have to be alone with his dark thoughts. He also says that she helps keep him organized and prepared for his classes at school.

   D. She goes to the cemetery with him each week to put fresh flowers on Robbie's grave. He also says she is the only one who listens to him.

C 4. What does Andy say in his letter to Rob's parents?

   A. He tells them he is considering suicide and admits it wasn't even his idea to help Rob.

   B. He admits he bought the beer and includes a photo of Rob from earlier that night.

   C. He asks for forgiveness and makes a list of all the good things he remembers about Rob.

   D. He tells them he is sorry and writes a short poem remembering Rob.

A 5. What does Andy say to Dr. Carrothers to convince the doctor that he has improved enough to have appointments on an as-needed basis?

   A. He says he's sleeping better and doing better in school. He admits he still blames himself but says that he is learning to live with the guilt.

   B. He says his has stopped thinking about suicide and is a happier person. He says he has forgiven himself and no longer feels guilty.

   C. He says he has improved his relationship with his parents and feels like he can talk to them now. He says he doesn't need a therapist because his parents can help him.

   D. He says his parents can no longer afford private therapy, and he will just talk with the school counselor unless things get bad again.

D 6. How does Andy's mother respond when Andy asks for help handling the accident? A. She tells him she doesn't know any way to help him and that he should talk to his dad.

   B. She tells him it's all her fault and that she should have realized he needed help sooner.

   C. She tells him she will do everything she can to help him, including coming home earlier to spend more time with him.

   D. She tells him that time will heal all wounds and that he's young and resilient so he will bounce back.

D 7. Which three people does Andy try to call before he kills himself, and what response does he get from each?

   A. He calls Rhonda, who is busy hanging out with Tyrone, Keisha, who is studying, and his coach, who is not at home.

   B. He tries to talk to his mom, who is working on stuff for the homeowners' group, his dad, who is working late at the office, and his brother, who is too young to understand.

   C. He calls Tyrone, who is out on a date with Rhonda, Keisha, who is still mad at him from the talent show, and B.J., who is at church.

   D. He calls Dr. Carrothers, who is out of town and cannot take the call, Keisha, whose mother answers and says she is asleep, and his basketball coach, who is not home.

B 8. What does Monty see on the ceiling?

    A. A note

    B. Blood

    C. A hole from the shotgun

    D. A noose

A 9. Why is Tyrone mad at the suicide prevention/grief counseling woman at their school? A. He is angry because he and B.J. went to the school counselor with their concerns about Andy and his depression, but no one did anything until it was too late.

    B. He is angry because he called the hotline, and no one ever contacted Andy to see if he was okay until two days after his suicide.

    C. He is angry because she is putting all the blame of Andy's suicide on the student body for not noticing his depression and trying to help.

    D. He is angry because she doesn't know how to help the student body deal with Andy's suicide. All her suggestions don't seem to help anyone feel better about what happened.

C 10. What does the grief counselor suggest Andy's friends should do to try to work through their pain and frustration over Andy's death?

    A. Attend a grief counseling seminar at the community outreach center

    B. Pray for help is dealing with the pain

    C. Write a letter to Andy explaining how they feel

    D. Share their feelings one at a time while others listen

IV. VOCABULARY

Q	1. HONORABLE	A. Distrusting or seeing the worst in the motives of others
J	2. VAST	B. Conscious or unconscious restraint of a behavior
F	3. UNRULY	C. Unable to be avoided or escaped; certain
O	4. TRIBUTE	D. Deal out; distribute
E	5. CAPABLE	E. Having ability
D	6. DISPENSE	F. Difficult or impossible to discipline or control
N	7. RIGHTEOUS	G. Actually; really; authentically
R	8. DENSE	H. A cause of loss, damage, disadvantage, or injury
L	9. COMMODITIES	I. Easily perceived or understood
A	10. CYNICAL	J. Very great in area or extent; immense
I	11. APPARENT	K. A useful and desirable thing or quality
C	12. INEVITABLE	L. Articles of trade or commerce; products
G	13. GENUINELY	M. Become a part of the main or dominant culture
B	14. INHIBITIONS	N. Acting in an upright, moral way; virtuous
T	15. INTENTIONS	O. An acknowledgment of gratitude, respect, or admiration
P	16. REPREHENSIBLE	P. Deserving of reproof, rebuke, or censure; blameworthy
S	17. PUNITIVE	Q. Deserving or winning respect or distinction
H	18. DETRIMENT	R. Difficult to understand or follow because of being closely packed with ideas or complexities of style
K	19. ASSET	S. Punishing
M	20. ASSIMILATE	T. Objectives; motives

Tears of a Tiger MULTIPLE CHOICE UNIT TEST 2

I. MATCHING

____ 1. GERALD   A. I knew better. We all did. We just never figured it would happen to __.

____ 2. TYRONE   B. What Rob's mother would always tell Andy he got for Christmas

____ 3. BJ   C. Carrothers

____ 4. LAW   D. Story Andy's class is reading when he runs out of the classroom.

____ 5. KEISHA   E. Andy may want to major in this.

____ 6. ROCK   F. B.J. and Tyrone go to see this person in hopes of helping Andy.

____ 7. NOTHING   G. ___'s home. ___ cares....I wish I could sleep forever.

____ 8. COUNSELOR   H. Andy thinks she loves him.

____ 9. PSYCHOLOGIST I. Andy's father brushes off her concerns.

____ 10. RHONDA   J. Rob's last name

____ 11. TEACHER   K. Keisha's best friend

____ 12. TIGER   L. Rhonda's most frightening moment: realizing that kids could ___

____ 13. MONTY   M. Invited but decides not to go out with the boys after the game

____ 14. PRAY   N. Andy's little brother

____ 15. MACBETH   O. No son of mine is going to be a ___!

____ 16. DIE   P. Helped Andy out of the car

____ 17. FAILURE   Q. What Andy says he sees in his future

____ 18. WASHINGTON   R. The only one not drinking the night of the accident

____ 19. NOBODY   S. BJ does this to help cope with the accident.

____ 20. US   T. Monty puts tears on this animal.

155

II. MULTIPLE CHOICE

1. How does Andy's personality change following the accident? What do his friends begin to notice about him?
    A. Andy hates hanging out with any of his old friends and tries to avoid them at all costs. They all say he has become mean.
    B. Andy likes to be alone a lot, and he has crying spells. They also say he is depressed.
    C. Andy never makes eye contact and has become quiet. They also say he seems more violent.
    D. Andy has become very outgoing and loud. They all noticed he seems to be trying to hide something.

2. How does Andy describe his relationship with his family to his psychologist?
    A. He says his parents fight all the time and make life hard for him and his brother. His father drinks and takes it out on the family, making his mother depressed. He feels like his home life is tough.
    B. He says his parents don't understand him at all. His father works all the time and his mother is out of touch with reality. He feels like they love his younger brother more than him.
    C. He says his parents are like any other parents. His father gets on his case from time to time, and his mother is very involved in his life. He just feels like any other average teenager with a normal family life.
    D. He says his parents are hard on him sometimes, but he knows it's because they love him. His father wants him to go to college and his mother encourages him to do his best in everything. He sometimes feels annoyed and pressured but ultimately knows they love him.

3. Why does Andy choose to let his grades slide?
    A. He says he can't focus on his school work because all he can think about is Rob, and no one understands what he is going through.
    B. He says his teachers make fun of him, his friends have abandoned him after the accident, and his parents are never home to help him when he needs it.
    C. He says his parents push him to be something he isn't, his friends make fun of him if he does well, and his teachers set very low expectations for black students like him.
    D. He says he already has rejection letters from four colleges, he has no money for college, and he has too much to deal with from the accident.

4. What promise does Dr. Carrothers make Andy agree to during their therapy session?

    A. That Andy will continue to stay in contact with Rob's parents until he sorts through all of his emotions

    B. That Andy will try to communicate with his father at least once a day and will try to build a better relationship with him

    C. That if Andy ever gets too depressed, he will call Dr. Carrothers before he tries to hurt himself

    D. That when Andy graduates from high school, he will pick a career that will help people instead of one that will make him a lot of money

5. When B.J. and Tyrone are concerned about Andy and go to talk to the school counselor about him, what is her response to their concerns?

    A. They should just give Andy his space and let him grieve in any way he needs.

    B. Andy is in high school and needs to learn how to deal with his own problems, so let him work it out on his own.

    C. They should talk to Andy and try to work through their problems together since they were all involved in the accident.

    D. Andy is getting counseling outside of school and not to worry, he's getting the help he needs.

6. Andy talks to his mother after the talent show, to try to explain to her how he feels. To what does he compare his feelings?

    A. Numbness

    B. Death

    C. Drowning

    D. A coma

7. Which three people does Andy try to call before he kills himself, and what response does he get from each?

    A. He calls Rhonda, who is busy hanging out with Tyrone, Keisha, who is studying, and his coach, who is not at home.

    B. He tries to talk to his mom, who is working on stuff for the homeowners' group, his dad, who is working late at the office, and his brother, who is too young to understand.

    C. He calls Dr. Carrothers, who is out of town and cannot take the call, Keisha, whose mother answers and says she is asleep, and his basketball coach, who is not home.

    D. He calls Tyrone, who is out on a date with Rhonda, Keisha, who is still mad at him from the talent show, and B.J., who is at church.

8. What does Monty see on the ceiling?

   A. A hole from the shotgun

   B. A note

   C. A noose

   D. Blood

9. Why is Tyrone mad at the suicide prevention/grief counseling woman at their school?

   A. He is angry because he called the hotline, and no one ever contacted Andy to see if he was okay until two days after his suicide.

   B. He is angry because she doesn't know how to help the student body deal with Andy's suicide. All her suggestions don't seem to help anyone feel better about what happened.

   C. He is angry because he and B.J. went to the school counselor with their concerns about Andy and his depression, but no one did anything until it was too late.

   D. He is angry because she is putting all the blame of Andy's suicide on the student body for not noticing his depression and trying to help.

10. How do Andy's friends react to his suicide?

    A. They are all depressed and upset. Tyrone and B.J. even consider committing suicide themselves from having to deal with the pain.

    B. They are all very upset and angry. They have a difficult time understanding why he did it and feel like he took a coward's way out.

    C. They are not very surprised. Most students knew Andy was suffering and his suicide didn't come as much of a shock.

    D. They are all stunned and don't know why it happened. Everyone at school thought Andy was completely happy.

III. QUOTATIONS: Explain the importance and meaning of the following quotations:

1. Last week I learned that kids my age could die. That was the most frightening moment I ever had. (RA1)

2. I coulda controlled the drinkin'. I knew better. We all did. We just never figured it would happen to us. (RA1)

3. Like the lady said in the poem--you mindin' your own black business and all this white stuff jus' takes over your life. And I ain't jus' talkin' 'bout snow!(RA3)

4. [Andy's Father] "Andrew, I know the accident was very traumatic for you. But you have to get beyond it and move on. You have to be strong and show that you are bigger than the problem." [Andy] "Yes, I know. You've told me that before. Be a man. Be strong. Put this 'unfortunate incident' behind you. Well, maybe I can't do that." (RA6)

5. So, I guess the pain is over for you now. You have moved to the place where there is no pain, and I guess that's good. But the pain left by your absence is like a wound in our hearts that will not heal. Nobody understands why you decided to end your life when you had so much to live for. So you're out of it and we have to stay here, feeling your pain as well as our own. It really isn't fair, you know. (RA6)

IV. VOCABULARY

____ 1. INFINITE   A. Distrusting or seeing the worst in the motives of others

____ 2. DIALECT   B. Of critical importance

____ 3. UNDIGNIFIED   C. A regional or social variety of a language distinguished by pronunciation, grammar, or vocabulary

____ 4. RECUPERATED   D. Punishing

____ 5. RIGHTEOUS   E. Difficult to understand or follow because of being closely packed with ideas or complexities of style

____ 6. FORTUNATE   F. Returned to health or strength; recovered

____ 7. DENSE   G. Acting in an upright, moral way; virtuous

____ 8. VITAL   H. Lacking respect and honor

____ 9. CYNICAL   I. Conscious or unconscious restraint of a behavior

____ 10. ELIMINATE   J. Deserving of reproof, rebuke, or censure; blameworthy

____ 11. PATIENT   K. Of ample or considerable amount

____ 12. DETERIORATION   L. To endure; to put up with

____ 13. CONFIDENCES   M. Not clearly; hazily; somewhat

____ 14. INHIBITIONS   N. Having calm endurance

____ 15. TOLERATE   O. Lucky

____ 16. VAGUELY   P. Immeasurably great or large; boundless

____ 17. REPREHENSIBLE   Q. Become a part of the main or dominant culture

____ 18. PUNITIVE   R. Feelings of assurance that a secret will be kept

____ 19. ASSIMILATE   S. The process of growing worse, weakening, or declining

____ 20. SUBSTANTIAL   T. To get rid of; remove

V. COMPOSITION

1. What is the significance of the title? (ALL)

2. How does the point of view enhance the novel? Give specific examples to support your answer. (ALL)

Tears of a Tiger MULTIPLE CHOICE UNIT TEST 2 Answer Key

I. MATCHING

M	1. GERALD	A. I knew better. We all did. We just never figured it would happen to __.
P	2. TYRONE	B. What Rob's mother would always tell Andy he got for Christmas
R	3. BJ	C. Carrothers
E	4. LAW	D. Story Andy's class is reading when he runs out of the classroom.
H	5. KEISHA	E. Andy may want to major in this.
B	6. ROCK	F. B.J. and Tyrone go to see this person in hopes of helping Andy.
Q	7. NOTHING	G. ___'s home. ___ cares....I wish I could sleep forever.
F	8. COUNSELOR	H. Andy thinks she loves him.
C	9. PSYCHOLOGIST	I. Andy's father brushes off her concerns.
K	10. RHONDA	J. Rob's last name
I	11. TEACHER	K. Keisha's best friend
T	12. TIGER	L. Rhonda's most frightening moment: realizing that kids could ___
N	13. MONTY	M. Invited but decides not to go out with the boys after the game
S	14. PRAY	N. Andy's little brother
D	15. MACBETH	O. No son of mine is going to be a ___!
L	16. DIE	P. Helped Andy out of the car
O	17. FAILURE	Q. What Andy says he sees in his future
J	18. WASHINGTON	R. The only one not drinking the night of the accident
G	19. NOBODY	S. BJ does this to help cope with the accident.
A	20. US	T. Monty puts tears on this animal.

II. MULTIPLE CHOICE

B 1. How does Andy's personality change following the accident? What do his friends begin to notice about him?

   A. Andy hates hanging out with any of his old friends and tries to avoid them at all costs. They all say he has become mean.

   B. Andy likes to be alone a lot, and he has crying spells. They also say he is depressed.

   C. Andy never makes eye contact and has become quiet. They also say he seems more violent.

   D. Andy has become very outgoing and loud. They all noticed he seems to be trying to hide something.

B 2. How does Andy describe his relationship with his family to his psychologist?

   A. He says his parents fight all the time and make life hard for him and his brother. His father drinks and takes it out on the family, making his mother depressed. He feels like his home life is tough.

   B. He says his parents don't understand him at all. His father works all the time and his mother is out of touch with reality. He feels like they love his younger brother more than him.

   C. He says his parents are like any other parents. His father gets on his case from time to time, and his mother is very involved in his life. He just feels like any other average teenager with a normal family life.

   D. He says his parents are hard on him sometimes, but he knows it's because they love him. His father wants him to go to college and his mother encourages him to do his best in everything. He sometimes feels annoyed and pressured but ultimately knows they love him.

C 3. Why does Andy choose to let his grades slide?

   A. He says he can't focus on his school work because all he can think about is Rob, and no one understands what he is going through.

   B. He says his teachers make fun of him, his friends have abandoned him after the accident, and his parents are never home to help him when he needs it.

   C. He says his parents push him to be something he isn't, his friends make fun of him if he does well, and his teachers set very low expectations for black students like him.

   D. He says he already has rejection letters from four colleges, he has no money for college, and he has too much to deal with from the accident.

C 4.   What promise does Dr. Carrothers make Andy agree to during their therapy session?

   A. That Andy will continue to stay in contact with Rob's parents until he sorts through all of his emotions

   B. That Andy will try to communicate with his father at least once a day and will try to build a better relationship with him

   C. That if Andy ever gets too depressed, he will call Dr. Carrothers before he tries to hurt himself

   D. That when Andy graduates from high school, he will pick a career that will help people instead of one that will make him a lot of money

D 5.   When B.J. and Tyrone are concerned about Andy and go to talk to the school counselor about him, what is her response to their concerns?

   A. They should just give Andy his space and let him grieve in any way he needs.

   B. Andy is in high school and needs to learn how to deal with his own problems, so let him work it out on his own.

   C. They should talk to Andy and try to work through their problems together since they were all involved in the accident.

   D. Andy is getting counseling outside of school and not to worry, he's getting the help he needs.

C 6.   Andy talks to his mother after the talent show, to try to explain to her how he feels. To what does he compare his feelings?

   A. Numbness

   B. Death

   C. Drowning

   D. A coma

C 7.   Which three people does Andy try to call before he kills himself, and what response does he get from each?

   A. He calls Rhonda, who is busy hanging out with Tyrone, Keisha, who is studying, and his coach, who is not at home.

   B. He tries to talk to his mom, who is working on stuff for the homeowners' group, his dad, who is working late at the office, and his brother, who is too young to understand.

   C. He calls Dr. Carrothers, who is out of town and cannot take the call, Keisha, whose mother answers and says she is asleep, and his basketball coach, who is not home.

   D. He calls Tyrone, who is out on a date with Rhonda, Keisha, who is still mad at him from the talent show, and B.J., who is at church.

D 8. What does Monty see on the ceiling?

A. A hole from the shotgun

B. A note

C. A noose

D. Blood

C 9. Why is Tyrone mad at the suicide prevention/grief counseling woman at their school?

A. He is angry because he called the hotline, and no one ever contacted Andy to see if he was okay until two days after his suicide.

B. He is angry because she doesn't know how to help the student body deal with Andy's suicide. All her suggestions don't seem to help anyone feel better about what happened.

C. He is angry because he and B.J. went to the school counselor with their concerns about Andy and his depression, but no one did anything until it was too late.

D. He is angry because she is putting all the blame of Andy's suicide on the student body for not noticing his depression and trying to help.

B 10. How do Andy's friends react to his suicide?

A. They are all depressed and upset. Tyrone and B.J. even consider committing suicide themselves from having to deal with the pain.

B. They are all very upset and angry. They have a difficult time understanding why he did it and feel like he took a coward's way out.

C. They are not very surprised. Most students knew Andy was suffering and his suicide didn't come as much of a shock.

D. They are all stunned and don't know why it happened. Everyone at school thought Andy was completely happy.

IV. VOCABULARY

P	1. INFINITE	A. Distrusting or seeing the worst in the motives of others
C	2. DIALECT	B. Of critical importance
H	3. UNDIGNIFIED	C. A regional or social variety of a language distinguished by pronunciation, grammar, or vocabulary
F	4. RECUPERATED	D. Punishing
G	5. RIGHTEOUS	E. Difficult to understand or follow because of being closely packed with ideas or complexities of style
O	6. FORTUNATE	F. Returned to health or strength; recovered
E	7. DENSE	G. Acting in an upright, moral way; virtuous
B	8. VITAL	H. Lacking respect and honor
A	9. CYNICAL	I. Conscious or unconscious restraint of a behavior
T	10. ELIMINATE	J. Deserving of reproof, rebuke, or censure; blameworthy
N	11. PATIENT	K. Of ample or considerable amount
S	12. DETERIORATION	L. To endure; to put up with
R	13. CONFIDENCES	M. Not clearly; hazily; somewhat
I	14. INHIBITIONS	N. Having calm endurance
L	15. TOLERATE	O. Lucky
M	16. VAGUELY	P. Immeasurably great or large; boundless
J	17. REPREHENSIBLE	Q. Become a part of the main or dominant culture
D	18. PUNITIVE	R. Feelings of assurance that a secret will be kept
Q	19. ASSIMILATE	S. The process of growing worse, weakening, or declining
K	20. SUBSTANTIAL	T. To get rid of; remove

UNIT RESOURCE MATERIALS

BULLETIN BOARD IDEAS *Tears of a Tiger*

1. Save one corner of the board for the best of students' *Tears of a Tiger* writing assignments.
2. Take one of the word search puzzles and copy it over in a large size on the bulletin board. Write the clue words to find on one side. Invite students prior to and after class to find the words and circle them on the bulletin board.
3. Write several of the most significant quotations from the book onto the board on brightly colored paper.
4. Make a bulletin board listing the vocabulary words for this unit. As you complete sections of the novel and discuss the vocabulary for each section, write the definitions on the bulletin board. (If your board is one students face frequently, it will help them learn the words.)
5. Post photos and information or magazine/newspaper articles about teens who have dealt with serious issues. Many teen magazines run feature stories on teenagers who have overcome difficult situations, and students would most likely enjoy articles from magazines they like to read.
6. Post articles from newspapers about teens injured or killed in car accidents related to drinking. Try to find articles that contain reactions from friends, family, or the community.
7. Create a bulletin board with a communication theme. Place facts, information, and tips for better communication between teens and parents.
8. Create a bulletin board about suicide prevention or recognizing the signs of depression. Provide some basic facts and info and give hotlines or website students can visit to get more information.
9. Make a bulletin board covering other teen issues. You could post facts/statistics on drinking, drugs, dropping out, pregnancy, rape, etc. Next to each group of statistics, print out colorful copies of young adult novel covers that deal with those issues. A list of suggested novels and the topics they cover is listed below.

    * Drugs: *Crank* by Ellen Hopkins, *Impulse* by Ellen Hopkins, *Go Ask Alice* edited by Dr. Beatrice Sparks
    * Cutting: *Cut* by Patricia McCormick
    * Eating Disorders: *Diary of an Anorexic Girl* by Morgan Menzie
    * Teen Pregnancy: *Make Lemonade* by Virginia Euwer Wolff
        Catalyst by Laurie Halse Anderson
    * Dropping Out: *Make Lemonade* by Virginia Euwer Wolff
    * Suicide: *Burn Journals* by Brent Runyon, *Impulse* by Ellen Hopkins
    * Violence against others: *Burned* by Ellen Hopkins
    * Rape: *Lovely Bones* by Alice Sebold, *Speak* by Laurie Halse Anderson

10. Make a bulletin board with colorful copies of other books Sharon Draper has written. Include a short tease to get students interested in her other novels.
11. Divide the board into sections and assign groups of students to create mini-bulletin boards regarding assigned issues related to the book.

RELATED TOPICS *Tears of a Tiger*

1. Depression
2. Traits Of Good (or Bad) Relationships
3. Effective Communication
4. Careers in Counseling
5. School Newspaper Production
6. Basketball
7. Funeral Rites
8. Coping With Death
9. Discrimination
10. Physical Abuse
11. Deadly Car Accidents
12. Under Age Drinking
13. Suicide
14. Writing Forms (dialogue, letters, poetry, etc.)

MORE ACTIVITIES *Tears of a Tiger*

1. Have students design a new book cover (front and back and inside flaps) for *Tears of a Tiger.*
2. Have students design a bulletin board (ready to be put up; not just sketched) for *Tears of a Tiger.*
3. Have students write out the characters in the book and cast famous actors and actress for a movie version of the novel. Instruct students to write a brief explanation as to why the actors/actresses they select would be perfect for the part.
4. Have students create a soundtrack for *Tears of a Tiger*. Have students burn a CD of the songs, design a CD cover, and include brief explanations as to why they selected each song.
5. Have students create a MySpace or Facebook profile for a character in the story. Encourage them to post a blog from the character's point of view and add comments from friends to make the page more authentic.
6. Have students conduct further research on teen psychology and present their findings to the class.
7. Have students write a continuation to the story. Ask them to write about what each character is doing five years after the story ends.
8. Have students write a letter to their parents. In this letter, ask them to analyze the way they communicate now, and offer suggestions for improvements.
9. Have students conduct additional research on teen issues. Prompt them to create a Power Point Presentation to display their research.
10. Have students write about a time they felt guilty for something that happened. Encourage them to think about how they got over their guilt and include this in their writing.
11. Have teens do research on the criminal justice system for teens. Have them compare and contrast Andy's sentence with the sentences of others who are tried for the same thing.
12. Have students do the writing assignments the students at Hazelwood High School must do for their English class (Most Frightening Moment, If I Could Change the World, The Importance of Friends, etc).
13. Have students write about whether or not being smart is cool. Have them compare and contrast their idea of intelligence with Andy's.
14. Have students do further research on discrimination in schools.
15. Andy's English class discusses symbolism in class one day. Have your students analyze prominent symbols in literature. Make sure they pay attention to what various colors symbolize as well.
16. Andy has to write a difficult letter to Rob's parents. Ask your students to write a letter to someone apologizing for something they have done.
17. Have your students write their own story with a variety of characters and media like in the novel.
18. Have students select a character from the book and complete the "I Am" poem from that character's point of view. (See the following handout.)
19. Have students read the second or third book in the Hazelwood High trilogy to see what happens to Andy's friends.

"I Am" Poem

Complete this "I am" poem. You may select any character from the book to do this poem about. Be sure to write from his or her point of view and think about the things he or she would feel. You may use some short one word answers, but do not make each line only a few words. You should try to provide support from the novel to really develop this poem so that it reveals information and insight about the character you select.

I am (2 characteristics your character has)
I wonder (something your character wonders)
I hear (something real or imaginary your character hears)
I see (something real or imaginary your character sees)
I want (something your character desires)
I am (the first line of the poem repeated)

I pretend (something your character pretends to do)
I feel (something real or imaginary your character feels emotionally)
I touch (something real or imaginary your character would touch physically)
I worry (something your characters worries about)
I cry (something that makes your character upset)
I am (the first line of the poem repeated)

I understand (something your character knows)
I say (something your character believes in)
I dream (something your character would dream about)
I try (something your character makes an effort to do)
I hope (something your character hopes for)
I am (the first line of the poem repeated)

UNIT WORD LIST *Tears of a Tiger*

No.	Word	Clue/Definition
1.	ABUSE	Gerald is a victim of this.
2.	ALCOHOL	The cause of the car accident
3.	ANDREW	What Andy's dad always calls his son
4.	BANDAIDS	Gerald would get rid of peanut butter, these, and $5 bills.
5.	BASKETBALL	Andy's father did not attend any of these games.
6.	BJ	The only one not drinking the night of the accident
7.	BLACK	One teacher thinks all _____ kids are tough.
8.	CAPTAIN	Andy gets this position on the team after Rob's death.
9.	CEILING	Monty wonders why there is blood on this.
10.	COLD	Andy is worried that Rob will be ___ underground.
11.	COLLEGE	Andy's father dreams of his son going to _____.
12.	COUNSELOR	B.J. and Tyrone go to see this person in hopes of helping Andy.
13.	COWARD	Andy's friends think he is a _____ for killing himself.
14.	DIE	Rhonda's most frightening moment: realizing that kids could ___
15.	DRAPER	Author of Tears of a Tiger
16.	DREAM	Rob haunts Andy in this.
17.	DROWNED	Andy tells his mother about a time when he was younger and almost _____.
18.	FAILURE	No son of mine is going to be a ___!
19.	FORGIVENESS	Andy asks Rob's parents for this.
20.	FRIENDS	Keisha says life without them would be boring and meaningless.
21.	GERALD	Invited but decides not to go out with the boys after the game
22.	GRAVE	Monty visits Andy there.
23.	HAZELWOOD	Name of the school: ___ High
24.	HOMICIDE	Andy is charged with DWI and vehicular _____.
25.	JEFFERSON	Andy's last name
26.	KEISHA	Andy thinks she loves him.
27.	LAW	Andy may want to major in this.
28.	LETTER	Andy sends this to Rob's parents at his psychologist's request.
29.	MACBETH	Story Andy's class is reading when he runs out of the classroom.
30.	MALL	Keisha is bored with Andy's depression & her mom picks her up there.

No.	Word	Clue/Definition
31.	MONTY	Andy's little brother
32.	MOVIES	Keisha is too busy to go there with Andy.
33.	NOBODY	___'s home. ___ cares....I wish I could sleep forever.
34.	NOTHING	What Andy says he sees in his future
35.	PAIN	So you're out of it and we have to stay here, feeling your ___ as well as our own.
36.	POEM	Even though Andy writes this, he doesn't turn it in for a grade.
37.	PRAY	BJ does this to help cope with the accident.
38.	PSYCHOLOGIST	Carrothers
39.	RACE	Topic of discussion after reading the poem about snow
40.	RHONDA	Keisha's best friend
41.	RIPLEY	Coach who tried to help Andy
42.	ROB	Trapped in the car and burns to death
43.	ROCK	What Rob's mother would always tell Andy he got for Christmas
44.	SCOUTS	They were looking for Andy, but he wasn't at school.
45.	SHOTGUN	Andy uses this to kill himself.
46.	TALENT	Keisha and Andy break up at the _____ show.
47.	TEACHER	Andy's father brushes off her concerns.
48.	THREE	Number of people Andy attempts to contact before he kills himself
49.	TIGER	Monty puts tears on this animal.
50.	TYRONE	Helped Andy out of the car
51.	US	I knew better. We all did. We just never figured it would happen to ___.
52.	WALL	The car hit this.
53.	WASHINGTON	Rob's last name
54.	WINTERS	One Thousand Nine Hundred Sixty-Eight ___

WORD SEARCH Tears Of A Tiger

```
R O C K S M O V I E S T G R A V E A N
T O L G C T T B R W V B Y Q L R X N C
I W B R O W H L L A F X K R W H B D D
G S D R U B X R A A C R E T O O G R J
E C S W T L W X E W C E I L I N G E K
R X B H S E C C C E J K S E X D E W J
V X R H O T F B O O K W H M N A U P E
B A S K E T B A L L U M A L L D S M F
T B L H T E G H D C B N R L P R S O F
A U J C S R B U B G O D S I L R D N E
L S P P O X Q J N P X W P E P S A T R
E E N O T H I N G D R E A M L L G Y S
N N Z E J N O B O D Y S I R R O E P O
T H G M D I E L J D Z Y N W D B R Y N
```

Andy is worried that Rob will be ___ underground. (4)
Andy may want to major in this. (3)
Andy sends this to Rob's parents at his psychologist's request. (6)
Andy thinks she loves him. (6)
Andy uses this to kill himself. (7)
Andy's father did not attend any of these games. (10)
Andy's friends think he is a ___ for killing himself. (6)
Andy's last name (9)
Andy's little brother (5)
BJ and Tyrone go to see this person in hopes of helping Andy. (9)
BJ does this to help cope with the accident. (4)
Coach who tried to help Andy (6)
Even though Andy writes this, he doesn't turn it in for a grade. (4)
Gerald is a victim of this. (5)
Helped Andy out of the car (6)
I knew better. We all did. We just never figured it would happen to __. (2)
Keisha and Andy break up at the ___ show. (6)
Keisha is bored with Andy's depression & her mom picks her up there. (4)
Keisha is too busy to go there with Andy. (6)
Keisha says life without them would be boring and meaningless. (7)
Keisha's best friend (6)
Monty puts tears on this animal. (5)
Monty visited Andy there. (5)
Monty wonders why there is blood on this. (7)
Number of people Andy tries to contact before he kills himself (5)
One teacher thinks all ___ kids are tough. (5)
Rhonda's most frightening moment: realizing that kids could ___ (3)
Rob haunts Andy in this. (5)
So you're out of it and we have to stay here, feeling your ___ as well as our own. (4)
The car hits this. (4)
The cause of the car accident (7)
The only one not drinking the night of the accident (2)
They were looking for Andy, but he wasn't at school. (6)
Topic of discussion after reading the snow poem (4)
Trapped in the car and burned to death (3)
What Andy says he sees in his future (7)
What Andy's dad always calls his son (6)
What Rob's mother would always tell Andy he got for Christmas (4)
___'s home. ___ cares....I wish I could sleep forever. (6)

WORD SEARCH ANSWER KEY Tears Of A Tiger

```
R  O  C  K  S  M  O  V  I  E  S  T  G  R  A  V  E  A
T  O        C     T     B  R              Y     R     N
I     B     O        H  L  A  F  K  R        H        D
G        U           R  A  C  R  E        O  O        R
E     S     T           E  W  C  E  I  L  I  N  G  E
R        H  S  E           C  E  K  S     E     D  E  W  J
            O  T              O     W  H     N  A  U     E
B  A  S  K  E  T  B  A  L  L  U  M  A  L  L  D  S  M  F
T  B  L        E  G     D  C     N  R  L  P     S  O  F
A  U     C     R     U        O     S  I  L  R     N  E
L  S     P  O        N              W  P  E  P  A  T  R
E  E  N  O  T  H  I  N  G  D  R  E  A  M  L  L     Y  S
N     E     N  O  B  O  D  Y           I     R  O     O
T        M  D  I  E  L  J              N        D  R  Y  N
```

Andy is worried that Rob will be ___ underground. (4)
Andy may want to major in this. (3)
Andy sends this to Rob's parents at his psychologist's request. (6)
Andy thinks she loves him. (6)
Andy uses this to kill himself. (7)
Andy's father did not attend any of these games. (10)
Andy's friends think he is a ___ for killing himself. (6)
Andy's last name (9)
Andy's little brother (5)
BJ and Tyrone go to see this person in hopes of helping Andy. (9)
BJ does this to help cope with the accident. (4)
Coach who tried to help Andy (6)
Even though Andy writes this, he doesn't turn it in for a grade. (4)
Gerald is a victim of this. (5)
Helped Andy out of the car (6)
I knew better. We all did. We just never figured it would happen to ___. (2)
Keisha and Andy break up at the ___ show. (6)
Keisha is bored with Andy's depression & her mom picks her up there. (4)
Keisha is too busy to go there with Andy. (6)
Keisha says life without them would be boring and meaningless. (7)
Keisha's best friend (6)
Monty puts tears on this animal. (5)
Monty visited Andy there. (5)
Monty wonders why there is blood on this. (7)
Number of people Andy tries to contact before he kills himself (5)
One teacher thinks all ___ kids are tough. (5)
Rhonda's most frightening moment: realizing that kids could ___ (3)
Rob haunts Andy in this. (5)
So you're out of it and we have to stay here, feeling your ___ as well as our own. (4)
The car hits this. (4)
The cause of the car accident (7)
The only one not drinking the night of the accident (2)
They were looking for Andy, but he wasn't at school. (6)
Topic of discussion after reading the snow poem (4)
Trapped in the car and burned to death (3)
What Andy says he sees in his future (7)
What Andy's dad always calls his son (6)
What Rob's mother would always tell Andy he got for Christmas (4)
___'s home. ___ cares....I wish I could sleep forever. (6)

CROSSWORD - Tears Of A Tiger

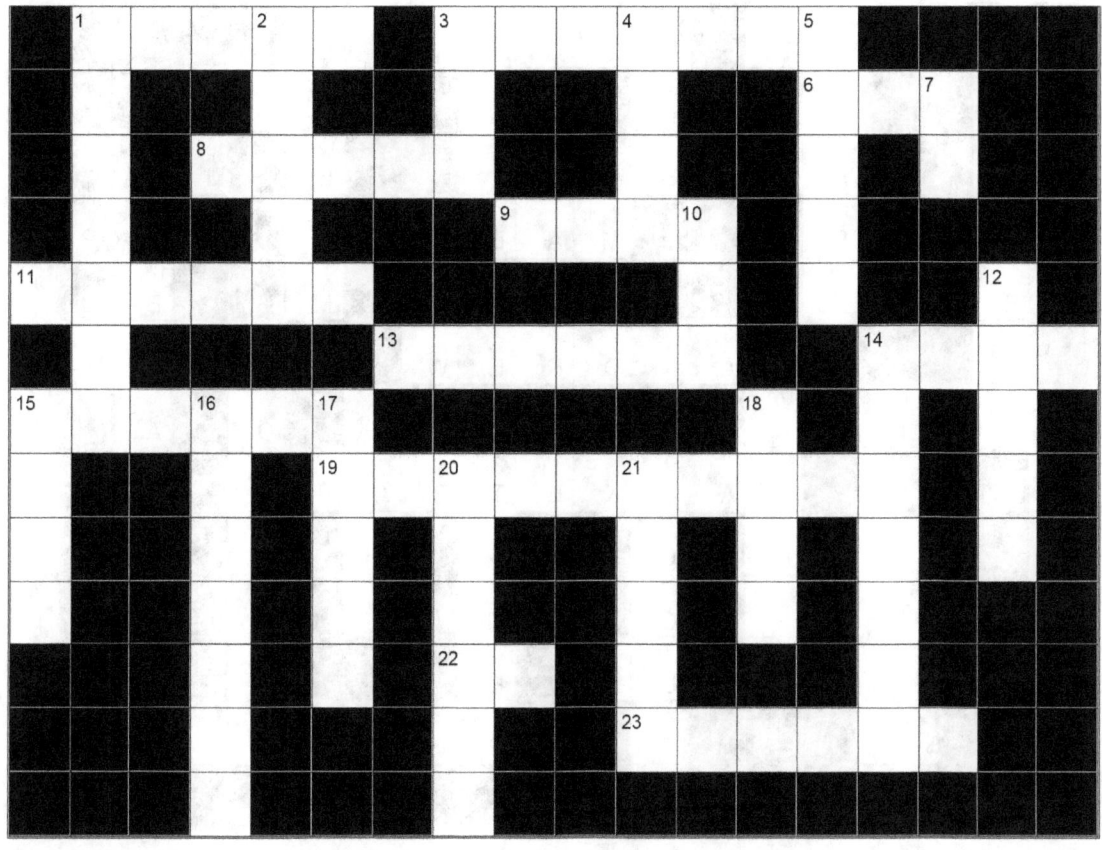

Across
1. Andy's little brother
3. Andy tells his mother about a time when he was younger and almost ___.
6. Trapped in the car and burned to death
8. Monty visited Andy there.
9. Keisha is bored with Andy's depression & her mom picks her up there.
11. Andy sends this to Rob's parents at his psychologist's request.
13. What Andy's dad always calls his son
14. Andy is worried that Rob will be ___ underground.
15. Keisha's best friend
19. Andy's father did not attend any of these games.
22. I knew better. We all did. We just never figured it would happen to __.
23. Coach who tried to help Andy

Down
1. Story Andy's class is reading when he runs out of the classroom
2. Number of people Andy tries to contact before he kills himself
3. Rhonda's most frightening moment: realizing that kids could ___
4. The car hits this.
5. Rob haunts Andy in this.
7. The only one not drinking the night of the accident
10. Andy may want to major in this.
12. One teacher thinks all ___ kids are tough.
14. Andy's father dreams of his son going to ___.
15. What Rob's mother would always tell Andy he got for Christmas
16. What Andy says he sees in his future
17. Gerald is a victim of this.
18. So you're out of it and we have to stay here, feeling your ___ as well as our own.
20. They were looking for Andy, but he wasn't at school.
21. Monty puts tears on this animal.

CROSSWORD ANSWER KEY - Tears Of A Tiger

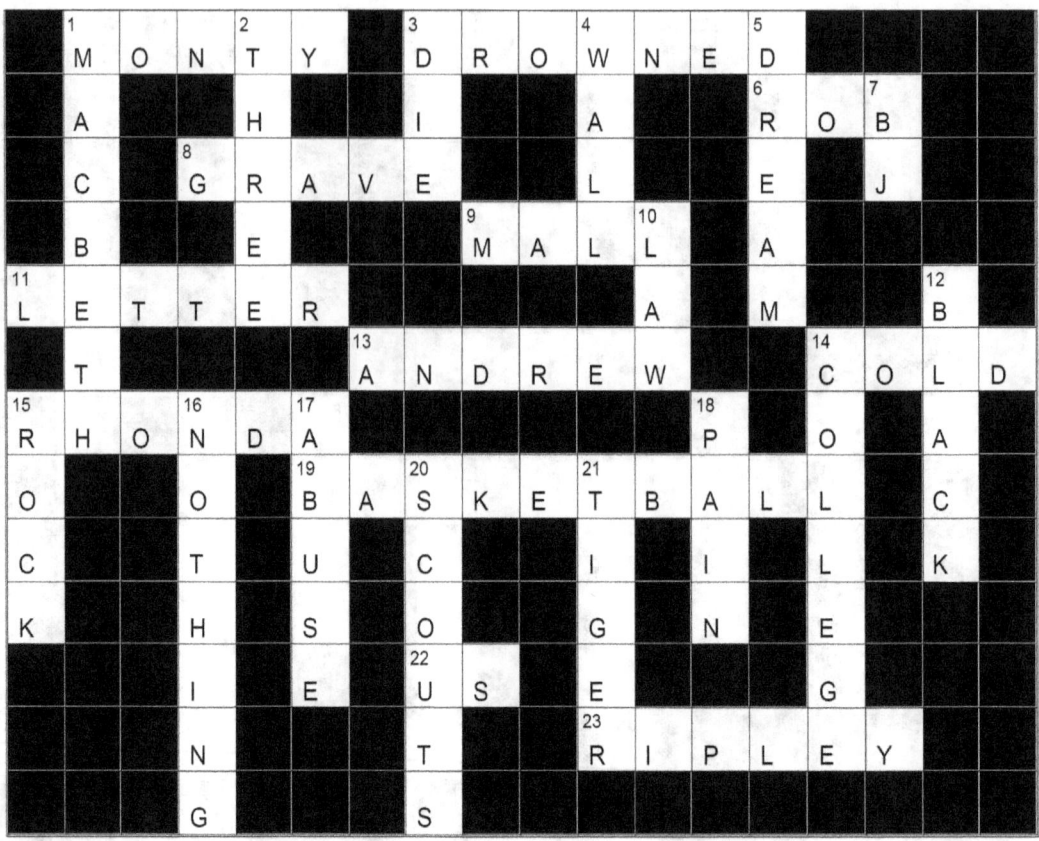

Across
1. Andy's little brother
3. Andy tells his mother about a time when he was younger and almost ___.
6. Trapped in the car and burned to death
8. Monty visited Andy there.
9. Keisha is bored with Andy's depression & her mom picks her up there.
11. Andy sends this to Rob's parents at his psychologist's request.
13. What Andy's dad always calls his son
14. Andy is worried that Rob will be ___ underground.
15. Keisha's best friend
19. Andy's father did not attend any of these games.
22. I knew better. We all did. We just never figured it would happen to __.
23. Coach who tried to help Andy

Down
1. Story Andy's class is reading when he runs out of the classroom
2. Number of people Andy tries to contact before he kills himself
3. Rhonda's most frightening moment: realizing that kids could ___
4. The car hits this.
5. Rob haunts Andy in this.
7. The only one not drinking the night of the accident
10. Andy may want to major in this.
12. One teacher thinks all ___ kids are tough.
14. Andy's father dreams of his son going to ___.
15. What Rob's mother would always tell Andy he got for Christmas
16. What Andy says he sees in his future
17. Gerald is a victim of this.
18. So you're out of it and we have to stay here, feeling your ___ as well as our own.
20. They were looking for Andy, but he wasn't at school.
21. Monty puts tears on this animal.

MATCHING 1 *Tears of a Tiger*

____ 1. MACBETH   A. Trapped in the car and burns to death

____ 2. KEISHA   B. Andy's father dreams of his son going to _____.

____ 3. LAW   C. The cause of the car accident

____ 4. FORGIVENESS   D. Monty wonders why there is blood on this.

____ 5. ROB   E. The only one not drinking the night of the accident

____ 6. CAPTAIN   F. Andy tells his mother about a time when he was younger and almost _____.

____ 7. BJ   G. What Andy's dad always calls his son

____ 8. TYRONE   H. Andy thinks she loves him.

____ 9. GERALD   I. Carrothers

____ 10. ROCK   J. What Rob's mother would always tell Andy he got for Christmas

____ 11. LETTER   K. Andy asks Rob's parents for this.

____ 12. CEILING   L. Invited but decides not to go out with the boys after the game

____ 13. ANDREW   M. Andy sends this to Rob's parents at his psychologist's request.

____ 14. COLLEGE   N. Story Andy's class is reading when he runs out of the classroom.

____ 15. DROWNED   O. Helped Andy out of the car

____ 16. BLACK   P. Andy may want to major in this.

____ 17. TIGER   Q. One teacher thinks all _____ kids are tough.

____ 18. PSYCHOLOGIST   R. Monty puts tears on this animal.

____ 19. COUNSELOR   S. B.J. and Tyrone go to see this person in hopes of helping Andy.

____ 20. ALCOHOL   T. Andy gets this position on the team after Rob's death.

MATCHING 1 ANSWER KEY *Tears of a Tiger*

N	1. MACBETH	A. Trapped in the car and burns to death
H	2. KEISHA	B. Andy's father dreams of his son going to _____.
P	3. LAW	C. The cause of the car accident
K	4. FORGIVENESS	D. Monty wonders why there is blood on this.
A	5. ROB	E. The only one not drinking the night of the accident
T	6. CAPTAIN	F. Andy tells his mother about a time when he was younger and almost _____.
E	7. BJ	G. What Andy's dad always calls his son
O	8. TYRONE	H. Andy thinks she loves him.
L	9. GERALD	I. Carrothers
J	10. ROCK	J. What Rob's mother would always tell Andy he got for Christmas
M	11. LETTER	K. Andy asks Rob's parents for this.
D	12. CEILING	L. Invited but decides not to go out with the boys after the game
G	13. ANDREW	M. Andy sends this to Rob's parents at his psychologist's request.
B	14. COLLEGE	N. Story Andy's class is reading when he runs out of the classroom.
F	15. DROWNED	O. Helped Andy out of the car
Q	16. BLACK	P. Andy may want to major in this.
R	17. TIGER	Q. One teacher thinks all _____ kids are tough.
I	18. PSYCHOLOGIST	R. Monty puts tears on this animal.
S	19. COUNSELOR	S. B.J. and Tyrone go to see this person in hopes of helping Andy.
C	20. ALCOHOL	T. Andy gets this position on the team after Rob's death.

MATCHING 2 *Tears of a Tiger*

____ 1. RIPLEY   A. Andy thinks she loves him.

____ 2. RACE   B. Andy's little brother

____ 3. POEM   C. The only one not drinking the night of the accident

____ 4. KEISHA   D. Rhonda's most frightening moment: realizing that kids could ___

____ 5. BASKETBALL   E. Andy gets this position on the team after Rob's death.

____ 6. DIE   F. ___'s home. ___ cares....I wish I could sleep forever.

____ 7. ROB   G. BJ does this to help cope with the accident.

____ 8. CAPTAIN   H. Coach who tried to help Andy

____ 9. BJ   I. Helped Andy out of the car

____ 10. NOTHING   J. Even though Andy writes this, he doesn't turn it in for a grade.

____ 11. PSYCHOLOGIST   K. Andy's last name

____ 12. NOBODY   L. Trapped in the car and burns to death

____ 13. JEFFERSON   M. Keisha's best friend

____ 14. COWARD   N. Carrothers

____ 15. PRAY   O. Topic of discussion after reading the poem about snow

____ 16. MONTY   P. Andy's father did not attend any of these games.

____ 17. ANDREW   Q. Andy's father brushes off her concerns.

____ 18. TEACHER   R. What Andy says he sees in his future

____ 19. RHONDA   S. What Andy's dad always calls his son

____ 20. TYRONE   T. Andy's friends think he is a _____ for killing himself.

MATCHING 2 ANSWER KEY *Tears of a Tiger*

H	1. RIPLEY	A. Andy thinks she loves him.
O	2. RACE	B. Andy's little brother
J	3. POEM	C. The only one not drinking the night of the accident
A	4. KEISHA	D. Rhonda's most frightening moment: realizing that kids could ___
P	5. BASKETBALL	E. Andy gets this position on the team after Rob's death.
D	6. DIE	F. ___'s home. ___ cares....I wish I could sleep forever.
L	7. ROB	G. BJ does this to help cope with the accident.
E	8. CAPTAIN	H. Coach who tried to help Andy
C	9. BJ	I. Helped Andy out of the car
R	10. NOTHING	J. Even though Andy writes this, he doesn't turn it in for a grade.
N	11. PSYCHOLOGIST	K. Andy's last name
F	12. NOBODY	L. Trapped in the car and burns to death
K	13. JEFFERSON	M. Keisha's best friend
T	14. COWARD	N. Carrothers
G	15. PRAY	O. Topic of discussion after reading the poem about snow
B	16. MONTY	P. Andy's father did not attend any of these games.
S	17. ANDREW	Q. Andy's father brushes off her concerns.
Q	18. TEACHER	R. What Andy says he sees in his future
M	19. RHONDA	S. What Andy's dad always calls his son
I	20. TYRONE	T. Andy's friends think he is a _____ for killing himself.

JUGGLE LETTERS 1 *Tears of a Tiger*

_____ = 1. ELRYPI
     Coach who tried to help Andy

_____ = 2. YETNOR
     Helped Andy out of the car

_____ = 3. OSVFNGERESI
     Andy asks Rob's parents for this.

_____ = 4. EHAIKS
     Andy thinks she loves him.

_____ = 5. NASDIABD
     Gerald would get rid of peanut butter, these, and $5 bills.

_____ = 6. TGNINHO
     What Andy says he sees in his future

_____ = 7. CORSNOEUL
     B.J. and Tyrone go to see this person in hopes of helping Andy.

_____ = 8. NDHARO
     Keisha's best friend

_____ = 9. WDOEDNR
     Andy tells his mother about a time when he was younger and almost _____.

_____ = 10. WRDEAN
     What Andy's dad always calls his son

_____ = 11. OYNMT
     Andy's little brother

_____ = 12. ECABTHM
     Story Andy's class is reading when he runs out of the classroom.

_____ = 13. ZOAOWELDH
     Name of the school: ___ High

_____ = 14. GNSAIOHNWT
     Rob's last name

_____ = 15. DERLGA
     Invited but decides not to go out with the boys after the game

JUGGLE LETTERS 1 ANSWER KEY *Tears of a Tiger*

RIPLEY = 1. ELRYPI
  Coach who tried to help Andy

TYRONE = 2. YETNOR
  Helped Andy out of the car

FORGIVENESS = 3. OSVFNGERESI
  Andy asks Rob's parents for this.

KEISHA = 4. EHAIKS
  Andy thinks she loves him.

BANDAIDS = 5. NASDIABD
  Gerald would get rid of peanut butter, these, and $5 bills.

NOTHING = 6. TGNINHO
  What Andy says he sees in his future

COUNSELOR = 7. CORSNOEUL
  B.J. and Tyrone go to see this person in hopes of helping Andy.

RHONDA = 8. NDHARO
  Keisha's best friend

DROWNED = 9. WDOEDNR
  Andy tells his mother about a time when he was younger and almost _____.

ANDREW = 10. WRDEAN
  What Andy's dad always calls his son

MONTY = 11. OYNMT
  Andy's little brother

MACBETH = 12. ECABTHM
  Story Andy's class is reading when he runs out of the classroom.

HAZELWOOD = 13. ZOAOWELDH
  Name of the school: ___ High

WASHINGTON = 14. GNSAIOHNWT
  Rob's last name

GERALD = 15. DERLGA
  Invited but decides not to go out with the boys after the game

JUGGLE LETTERS 2 *Tears of a Tiger*

_____ = 1. BONYDO
   ___'s home. ___ cares....I wish I could sleep forever.

_____ = 2. JB
   The only one not drinking the night of the accident

_____ = 3. TIAANPC
   Andy gets this position on the team after Rob's death.

_____ = 4. NIERSFD
   Keisha says life without them would be boring and meaningless.

_____ = 5. KCRO
   What Rob's mother would always tell Andy he got for Christmas

_____ = 6. EARC
   Topic of discussion after reading the poem about snow

_____ = 7. TRELET
   Andy sends this to Rob's parents at his psychologist's request.

_____ = 8. DEARM
   Rob haunts Andy in this.

_____ = 9. OUNSRCEOL
   B.J. and Tyrone go to see this person in hopes of helping Andy.

_____ = 10. GPOCHOYSTISL
   Carrothers

_____ = 11. RHDANO
   Keisha's best friend

_____ = 12. THRCEAE
   Andy's father brushes off her concerns.

_____ = 13. CGIENLI
   Monty wonders why there is blood on this.

_____ = 14. OWDCRA
   Andy's friends think he is a _____ for killing himself.

_____ = 15. RDAELG
   Invited but decides not to go out with the boys after the game

JUGGLE LETTERS 2 ANSWER KEY *Tears of a Tiger*

NOBODY	= 1. BONYDO
	___'s home. ___ cares....I wish I could sleep forever.
BJ	= 2. JB
	The only one not drinking the night of the accident
CAPTAIN	= 3. TIAANPC
	Andy gets this position on the team after Rob's death.
FRIENDS	= 4. NIERSFD
	Keisha says life without them would be boring and meaningless.
ROCK	= 5. KCRO
	What Rob's mother would always tell Andy he got for Christmas
RACE	= 6. EARC
	Topic of discussion after reading the poem about snow
LETTER	= 7. TRELET
	Andy sends this to Rob's parents at his psychologist's request.
DREAM	= 8. DEARM
	Rob haunts Andy in this.
COUNSELOR	= 9. OUNSRCEOL
	B.J. and Tyrone go to see this person in hopes of helping Andy.
PSYCHOLOGIST	= 10. GPOCHOYSTISL
	Carrothers
RHONDA	= 11. RHDANO
	Keisha's best friend
TEACHER	= 12. THRCEAE
	Andy's father brushes off her concerns.
CEILING	= 13. CGIENLI
	Monty wonders why there is blood on this.
COWARD	= 14. OWDCRA
	Andy's friends think he is a _____ for killing himself.
GERALD	= 15. RDAELG
	Invited but decides not to go out with the boys after the game

VOCABULARY RESOURCE MATERIALS

This page is left blank for two-sided printing.

Tears of a Tiger Vocabulary

No. Word	Clue/Definition
1. ACCUSTOMED	In the habit of; used to
2. APPARENT	Easily perceived or understood
3. ASPECTS	Parts; features; phases
4. ASSET	A useful and desirable thing or quality
5. ASSIMILATE	Become a part of the main or dominant culture
6. ASSURED	Guaranteed; sure; certain
7. BOMBARD	To attack or assail, as with artillery or rapid fire
8. CAPABLE	Having ability
9. COMMODITIES	Articles of trade or commerce; products
10. CONFIDENCES	Feelings of assurance that a secret will be kept
11. CONVERT	Persuade to adopt a particular belief
12. CYNICAL	Distrusting or seeing the worst in the motives of others
13. DENSE	Difficult to understand or follow because of being closely packed with ideas or complexities of style
14. DESIRE	A longing for; wanting
15. DETERIORATION	The process of growing worse, weakening, or declining
16. DETRIMENT	A cause of loss, damage, disadvantage, or injury
17. DIALECT	A regional or social variety of a language distinguished by pronunciation, grammar, or vocabulary
18. DISPENSE	Deal out; distribute
19. DISTURBANCES	Outbreaks of disorder; commotion
20. ELIMINATE	To get rid of; remove
21. FORTUNATE	Lucky
22. FRENZIED	Wildly excited or enthusiastic
23. GENUINELY	Actually; really; authentically
24. GRIEVING	Experiencing or expressing sorrow
25. HECTIC	Characterized by intense activity, confusion, or haste
26. HONORABLE	Deserving or winning respect or distinction
27. IMPLANTS	Sets securely in place
28. INCIDENTS	Minor events
29. INEVITABLE	Unable to be avoided or escaped; certain
30. INFINITE	Immeasurably great or large; boundless
31. INHIBITIONS	Conscious or unconscious restraint of a behavior
32. INTENTIONS	Objectives; motives
33. INTRUDE	To put or force in inappropriately, especially without permission

No.	Word	Clue/Definition
34.	PATIENT	Having calm endurance
35.	PUNITIVE	Punishing
36.	REBELLIOUS	Going against control or authority
37.	RECUPERATED	Returned to health or strength; recovered
38.	REMARKABLE	Worthy of notice or attention
39.	REPREHENSIBLE	Deserving of reproof, rebuke, or censure; blameworthy
40.	REVELATION	An enlightening or astonishing disclosure
41.	RIGHTEOUS	Acting in an upright, moral way; virtuous
42.	SEVERITY	Intensity or sharpness
43.	SUBSTANTIAL	Of ample or considerable amount
44.	SUICIDE	The act of intentionally killing oneself
45.	TOLERATE	To endure; to put up with
46.	TRIBUTE	An acknowledgment of gratitude, respect, or admiration
47.	UNDIGNIFIED	Lacking respect and honor
48.	UNRULY	Difficult or impossible to discipline or control
49.	VAGUELY	Not clearly; hazily; somewhat
50.	VAST	Very great in area or extent; immense
51.	VERBALIZE	To express in words
52.	VITAL	Of critical importance

VOCABULARY WORD SEARCH - Tears Of A Tiger

```
A  S  S  U  R  E  D  R  E  B  E  L  L  I  O  U  S  R  D
P  C  O  M  M  O  D  I  T  I  E  S  Z  C  S  X  A  E  I
U  I  N  T  R  U  D  E  R  W  L  H  X  O  R  R  S  P  A
N  R  E  M  A  R  K  A  B  L  E  B  H  N  P  I  S  R  L
I  I  Q  W  D  I  S  P  E  N  S  E  M  V  A  N  I  E  E
T  H  N  Z  E  R  B  I  F  U  Z  N  T  E  C  M  H  H  C
I  Z  Z  H  S  N  K  M  M  R  N  H  T  R  I  I  I  E  T
V  A  S  T  I  R  E  C  U  P  E  R  A  T  E  D  L  N  H
E  I  C  C  R  B  V  N  A  G  L  N  U  S  N  E  A  S  O
A  L  T  Y  E  C  I  M  B  P  S  A  Z  L  T  N  T  I  N
S  D  A  A  H  E  C  T  I  C  A  P  N  I  Y  T  E  B  O
P  R  S  W  L  F  L  Q  I  H  D  B  B  T  E  S  V  L  R
E  R  S  U  I  C  I  D  E  O  E  Q  L  R  S  D  L  E  A
C  D  E  T  R  I  M  E  N  T  N  M  P  E  L  B  G  F  B
T  F  T  B  O  M  B  A  R  D  S  S  C  Y  N  I  C  A  L
S  V  A  G  U  E  L  Y  T  V  E  R  B  A  L  I  Z  E  E
```

ASPECTS	IMPLANTS
ASSET	INCIDENTS
ASSIMILATE	INHIBITIONS
ASSURED	INTRUDE
BOMBARD	PATIENT
CAPABLE	PUNITIVE
COMMODITIES	REBELLIOUS
CONVERT	RECUPERATED
CYNICAL	REMARKABLE
DENSE	REPREHENSIBLE
DESIRE	SUICIDE
DETRIMENT	UNRULY
DIALECT	VAGUELY
DISPENSE	VAST
FRENZIED	VERBALIZE
HECTIC	VITAL
HONORABLE	

VOCABULARY WORD SEARCH ANSWER KEY - Tears Of A Tiger

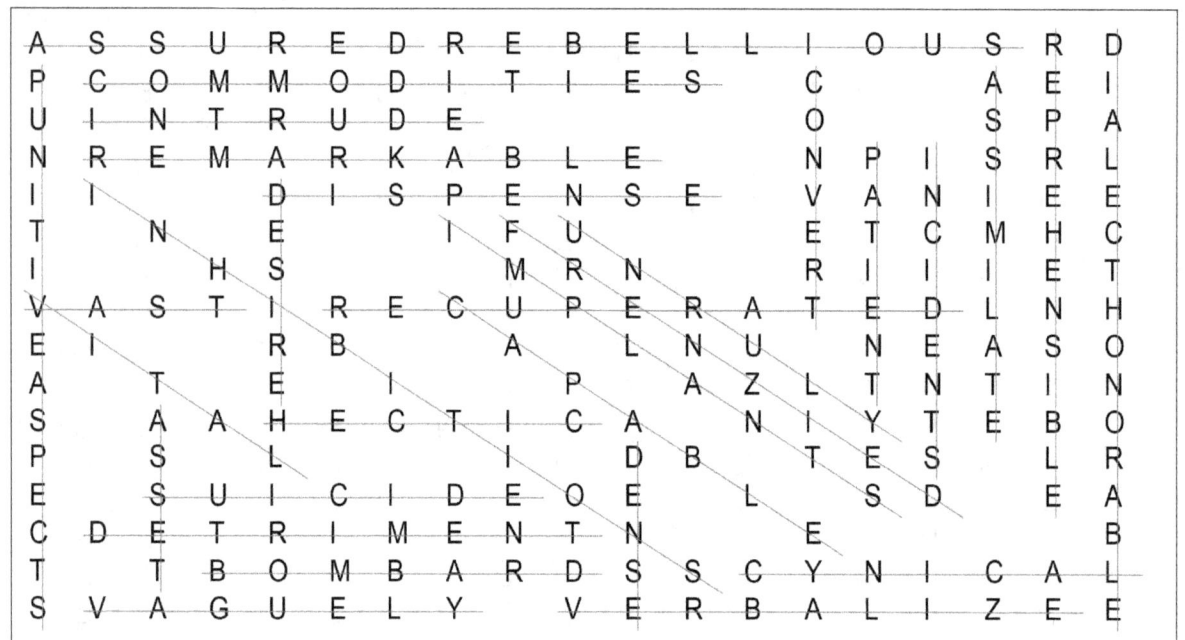

ASPECTS
ASSET
ASSIMILATE
ASSURED
BOMBARD
CAPABLE
COMMODITIES
CONVERT
CYNICAL
DENSE
DESIRE
DETRIMENT
DIALECT
DISPENSE
FRENZIED
HECTIC
HONORABLE

IMPLANTS
INCIDENTS
INHIBITIONS
INTRUDE
PATIENT
PUNITIVE
REBELLIOUS
RECUPERATED
REMARKABLE
REPREHENSIBLE
SUICIDE
UNRULY
VAGUELY
VAST
VERBALIZE
VITAL

VOCABULARY CROSSWORD - *Tears Of A Tiger*

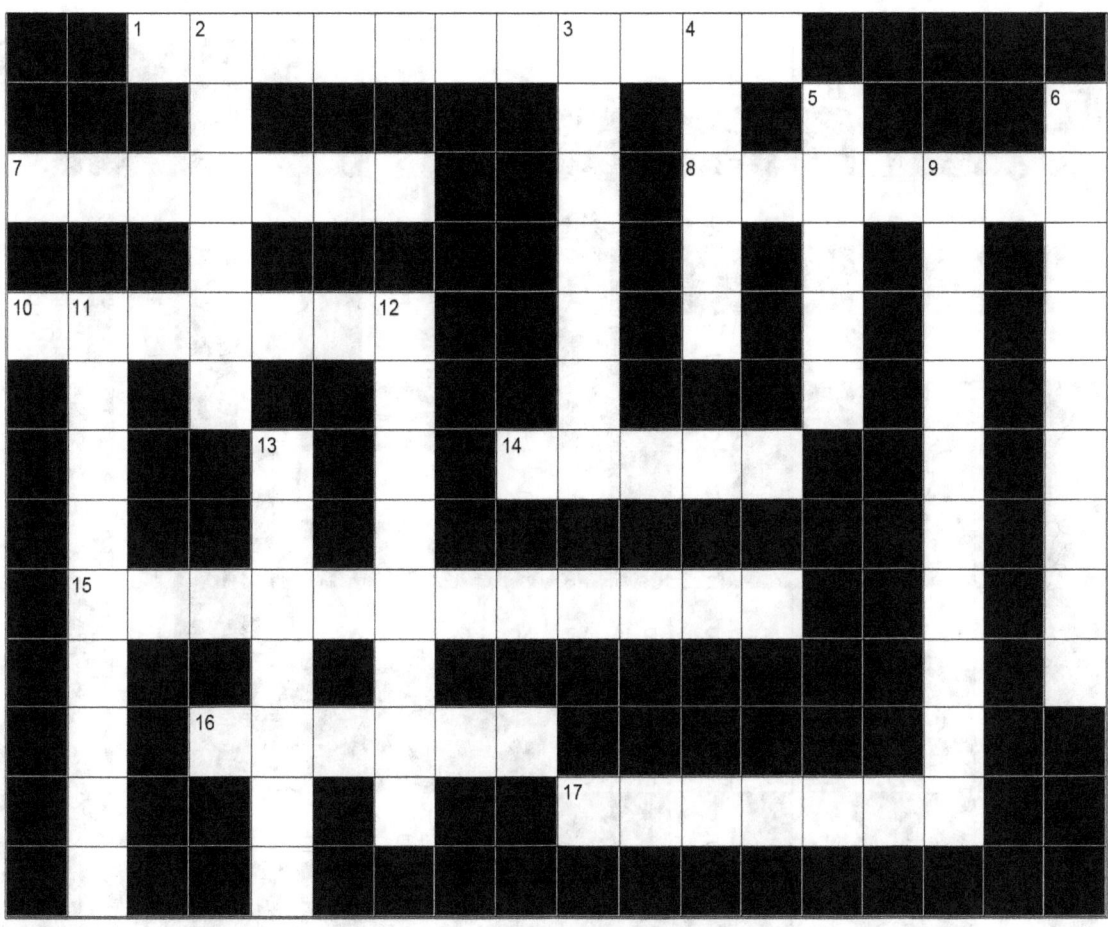

Across
1. Of ample or considerable amount
7. Put or force in inappropriately, especially without permission
8. The act of intentionally killing oneself
10. Regional or social variety of a language
14. Difficult to understand or follow because of being closely packed with ideas or complex styles
15. Outbreaks of disorder; commotion
16. Characterized by intense activity, confusion, or haste
17. Parts; features; phases

Down
2. Difficult or impossible to discipline or control
3. An acknowledgment of gratitude, respect, or admiration
4. A useful and desirable thing or quality
5. Of critical importance
6. To express in words
9. Objectives; motives
11. Minor events
12. To endure; to put up with
13. Having calm endurance

VOCABULARY CROSSWORD ANSWER KEY - *Tears Of A Tiger*

Across
1. Of ample or considerable amount
7. Put or force in inappropriately, especially without permission
8. The act of intentionally killing oneself
10. Regional or social variety of a language
14. Difficult to understand or follow because of being closely packed with ideas or complex styles
15. Outbreaks of disorder; commotion
16. Characterized by intense activity, confusion, or haste
17. Parts; features; phases

Down
2. Difficult or impossible to discipline or control
3. An acknowledgment of gratitude, respect, or admiration
4. A useful and desirable thing or quality
5. Of critical importance
6. To express in words
9. Objectives; motives
11. Minor events
12. To endure; to put up with
13. Having calm endurance

VOCABULARY MATCHING 1 *Tears of a Tiger*

____ 1. RECUPERATED   A. Become a part of the main or dominant culture

____ 2. ASSIMILATE   B. In the habit of; used to

____ 3. APPARENT   C. Easily perceived or understood

____ 4. ACCUSTOMED   D. Articles of trade or commerce; products

____ 5. REPREHENSIBLE   E. Wildly excited or enthusiastic

____ 6. REVELATION   F. Conscious or unconscious restraint of a behavior

____ 7. SUBSTANTIAL   G. Deserving of reproof, rebuke, or censure; blameworthy

____ 8. TOLERATE   H. A cause of loss, damage, disadvantage, or injury

____ 9. VAST   I. An enlightening or astonishing disclosure

____ 10. BOMBARD   J. To endure; to put up with

____ 11. CAPABLE   K. Having ability

____ 12. INHIBITIONS   L. Unable to be avoided or escaped; certain

____ 13. INEVITABLE   M. Of ample or considerable amount

____ 14. FRENZIED   N. Of critical importance

____ 15. ELIMINATE   O. Outbreaks of disorder; commotion

____ 16. DISTURBANCES   P. The process of growing worse, weakening, or declining

____ 17. DETRIMENT   Q. Returned to health or strength; recovered

____ 18. DETERIORATION   R. To get rid of; remove

____ 19. COMMODITIES   S. To attack or assail, as with artillery or rapid fire

____ 20. VITAL   T. Very great in area or extent; immense

VOCABULARY MATCHING 1 ANSWER KEY *Tears of a Tiger*

Q	1. RECUPERATED	A. Become a part of the main or dominant culture
A	2. ASSIMILATE	B. In the habit of; used to
C	3. APPARENT	C. Easily perceived or understood
B	4. ACCUSTOMED	D. Articles of trade or commerce; products
G	5. REPREHENSIBLE	E. Wildly excited or enthusiastic
I	6. REVELATION	F. Conscious or unconscious restraint of a behavior
M	7. SUBSTANTIAL	G. Deserving of reproof, rebuke, or censure; blameworthy
J	8. TOLERATE	H. A cause of loss, damage, disadvantage, or injury
T	9. VAST	I. An enlightening or astonishing disclosure
S	10. BOMBARD	J. To endure; to put up with
K	11. CAPABLE	K. Having ability
F	12. INHIBITIONS	L. Unable to be avoided or escaped; certain
L	13. INEVITABLE	M. Of ample or considerable amount
E	14. FRENZIED	N. Of critical importance
R	15. ELIMINATE	O. Outbreaks of disorder; commotion
O	16. DISTURBANCES	P. The process of growing worse, weakening, or declining
H	17. DETRIMENT	Q. Returned to health or strength; recovered
P	18. DETERIORATION	R. To get rid of; remove
D	19. COMMODITIES	S. To attack or assail, as with artillery or rapid fire
N	20. VITAL	T. Very great in area or extent; immense

VOCABULARY MATCHING 2 *Tears of a Tiger*

____ 1. VERBALIZE   A. Characterized by intense activity, confusion, or haste

____ 2. HECTIC   B. Deal out; distribute

____ 3. GRIEVING   C. Not clearly; hazily; somewhat

____ 4. FORTUNATE   D. Lacking respect and honor

____ 5. DISPENSE   E. Immeasurably great or large; boundless

____ 6. DIALECT   F. To express in words

____ 7. CYNICAL   G. Feelings of assurance that a secret will be kept

____ 8. CONFIDENCES   H. Punishing

____ 9. ASSURED   I. Sets securely in place

____ 10. IMPLANTS   J. The act of intentionally killing oneself

____ 11. INFINITE   K. Lucky

____ 12. VAGUELY   L. Going against control or authority

____ 13. UNDIGNIFIED   M. Guaranteed; sure; certain

____ 14. TRIBUTE   N. A regional or social variety of a language distinguished by pronunciation, grammar, or vocabulary

____ 15. SUICIDE   O. Experiencing or expressing sorrow

____ 16. SEVERITY   P. An acknowledgment of gratitude, respect, or admiration

____ 17. REBELLIOUS   Q. Distrusting or seeing the worst in the motives of others

____ 18. PUNITIVE   R. Having calm endurance

____ 19. PATIENT   S. Intensity or sharpness

____ 20. ASPECTS   T. Parts; features; phases

VOCABULARY MATCHING 2 ANSWER KEY *Tears of a Tiger*

F	1. VERBALIZE		A. Characterized by intense activity, confusion, or haste
A	2. HECTIC		B. Deal out; distribute
O	3. GRIEVING		C. Not clearly; hazily; somewhat
K	4. FORTUNATE		D. Lacking respect and honor
B	5. DISPENSE		E. Immeasurably great or large; boundless
N	6. DIALECT		F. To express in words
Q	7. CYNICAL		G. Feelings of assurance that a secret will be kept
G	8. CONFIDENCES		H. Punishing
M	9. ASSURED		I. Sets securely in place
I	10. IMPLANTS		J. The act of intentionally killing oneself
E	11. INFINITE		K. Lucky
C	12. VAGUELY		L. Going against control or authority
D	13. UNDIGNIFIED		M. Guaranteed; sure; certain
P	14. TRIBUTE		N. A regional or social variety of a language distinguished by pronunciation, grammar, or vocabulary
J	15. SUICIDE		O. Experiencing or expressing sorrow
S	16. SEVERITY		P. An acknowledgment of gratitude, respect, or admiration
L	17. REBELLIOUS		Q. Distrusting or seeing the worst in the motives of others
H	18. PUNITIVE		R. Having calm endurance
R	19. PATIENT		S. Intensity or sharpness
T	20. ASPECTS		T. Parts; features; phases

VOCABULARY JUGGLE LETTERS 1 *Tears of a Tiger*

_____ = 1. TRITUBE
   An acknowledgment of gratitude, respect, or admiration

_____ = 2. IIELMTNEA
   To get rid of; remove

_____ = 3. ESEISNPD
   Deal out; distribute

_____ = 4. TETNMDIER
   A cause of loss, damage, disadvantage, or injury

_____ = 5. LAICNYC
   Distrusting or seeing the worst in the motives of others

_____ = 6. OEDCFEINNCS
   Feelings of assurance that a secret will be kept

_____ = 7. AELPBAC
   Having ability

_____ = 8. SRDUAES
   Guaranteed; sure; certain

_____ = 9. ESSTA
   A useful and desirable thing or quality

_____ = 10. EFEZDIRN
   Wildly excited or enthusiastic

_____ = 11. RENVIGIG
   Experiencing or expressing sorrow

_____ = 12. EIYSTEVR
   Intensity or sharpness

_____ = 13. NIOAELVRTE
   An enlightening or astonishing disclosure

_____ = 14. BREAAKRLME
   Worthy of notice or attention

_____ = 15. RIBLESEULO
   Going against control or authority

_____ = 16. ENSNOITTIN
   Objectives; motives

_____ = 17. ITBIINNISHO
   Conscious or unconscious restraint of a behavior

_____ = 18. BAVNLTIEIE
   Unable to be avoided or escaped; certain

_____ = 19. EBLHAONRO
   Deserving or winning respect or distinction

_____ = 20. TUMCACEODS
   In the habit of; used to

VOCABULARY JUGGLE LETTERS 1 ANSWER KEY *Tears of a Tiger*

TRIBUTE	= 1. TRITUBE
	An acknowledgment of gratitude, respect, or admiration
ELIMINATE	= 2. IIELMTNEA
	To get rid of; remove
DISPENSE	= 3. ESEISNPD
	Deal out; distribute
DETRIMENT	= 4. TETNMDIER
	A cause of loss, damage, disadvantage, or injury
CYNICAL	= 5. LAICNYC
	Distrusting or seeing the worst in the motives of others
CONFIDENCES	= 6. OEDCFEINNCS
	Feelings of assurance that a secret will be kept
CAPABLE	= 7. AELPBAC
	Having ability
ASSURED	= 8. SRDUAES
	Guaranteed; sure; certain
ASSET	= 9. ESSTA
	A useful and desirable thing or quality
FRENZIED	= 10. EFEZDIRN
	Wildly excited or enthusiastic
GRIEVING	= 11. RENVIGIG
	Experiencing or expressing sorrow
SEVERITY	= 12. EIYSTEVR
	Intensity or sharpness
REVELATION	= 13. NIOAELVRTE
	An enlightening or astonishing disclosure
REMARKABLE	= 14. BREAAKRLME
	Worthy of notice or attention
REBELLIOUS	= 15. RIBLESEULO
	Going against control or authority
INTENTIONS	= 16. ENSNOITTIN
	Objectives; motives
INHIBITIONS	= 17. ITBIINNISHO
	Conscious or unconscious restraint of a behavior
INEVITABLE	= 18. BAVNLTIEIE
	Unable to be avoided or escaped; certain
HONORABLE	= 19. EBLHAONRO
	Deserving or winning respect or distinction
ACCUSTOMED	= 20. TUMCACEODS
	In the habit of; used to

VOCABULARY JUGGLE LETTERS 2 *Tears of a Tiger*

_____   = 1. LVAUEGY
   Not clearly; hazily; somewhat

_____   = 2. PNASMITL
   Sets securely in place

_____   = 3. NUYGEELIN
   Actually; really; authentically

_____   = 4. USNREBDCIAST
   Outbreaks of disorder; commotion

_____   = 5. LCTDIAE
   A regional or social variety of a language distinguished by pronunciation, grammar, or vocabulary

_____   = 6. OIOARNIETDTRE
   The process of growing worse, weakening, or declining

_____   = 7. DTESOMICMOI
   Articles of trade or commerce; products

_____   = 8. MBRBADO
   To attack or assail, as with artillery or rapid fire

_____   = 9. IALISMSTEA
   Become a part of the main or dominant culture

_____   = 10. SINDNECIT
   Minor events

_____   = 11. SNITNENTIO
   Objectives; motives

_____   = 12. IGFUIIDNDEN
   Lacking respect and honor

_____   = 13. LEAETOTR
   To endure; to put up with

_____   = 14. TUAASLBSNIT
   Of ample or considerable amount

_____   = 15. RIOHTGUES
   Acting in an upright, moral way; virtuous

_____   = 16. BEIRENHESLEPR
   Deserving of reproof, rebuke, or censure; blameworthy

_____   = 17. TUDRCERAPEE
   Returned to health or strength; recovered

_____   = 18. UTNIEPIV
   Punishing

_____   = 19. RNUIETD
   To put or force in inappropriately, especially without permission

_____   = 20. SATEPCS
   Parts; features; phases

VOCABULARY JUGGLE LETTERS 2 ANSWER KEY *Tears of a Tiger*

VAGUELY	= 1. LVAUEGY
	Not clearly; hazily; somewhat
IMPLANTS	= 2. PNASMITL
	Sets securely in place
GENUINELY	= 3. NUYGEELIN
	Actually; really; authentically
DISTURBANCES	= 4. USNREBDCIAST
	Outbreaks of disorder; commotion
DIALECT	= 5. LCTDIAE
	A regional or social variety of a language distinguished by pronunciation, grammar, or vocabulary
DETERIORATION	= 6. OIOARNIETDTRE
	The process of growing worse, weakening, or declining
COMMODITIES	= 7. DTESOMICMOI
	Articles of trade or commerce; products
BOMBARD	= 8. MBRBADO
	To attack or assail, as with artillery or rapid fire
ASSIMILATE	= 9. IALISMSTEA
	Become a part of the main or dominant culture
INCIDENTS	= 10. SINDNECIT
	Minor events
INTENTIONS	= 11. SNITNENTIO
	Objectives; motives
UNDIGNIFIED	= 12. IGFUIIDNDEN
	Lacking respect and honor
TOLERATE	= 13. LEAETOTR
	To endure; to put up with
SUBSTANTIAL	= 14. TUAASLBSNIT
	Of ample or considerable amount
RIGHTEOUS	= 15. RIOHTGUES
	Acting in an upright, moral way; virtuous
REPREHENSIBLE	= 16. BEIRENHESLEPR
	Deserving of reproof, rebuke, or censure; blameworthy
RECUPERATED	= 17. TUDRCERAPEE
	Returned to health or strength; recovered
PUNITIVE	= 18. UTNIEPIV
	Punishing
INTRUDE	= 19. RNUIETD
	To put or force in inappropriately, especially without permission
ASPECTS	= 20. SATEPCS
	Parts; features; phases

www.ingramcontent.com/pod-product-compliance
Lightning Source LLC
Chambersburg PA
CBHW051405070526
44584CB00023B/3295